EARTH, MY LIKENESS

Nature Poetry of Walt Whitman

Edited by Howard Nelson

HERON DANCE
PRESS

HΞRON DANCΞ PRΞ55
179 Rotax Road
N. Ferrisburg, VT 05473
www.herondance.org

Printed and bound in the United States.

Cover art and watercolors by Roderick MacIver of *Heron Dance*.

This book printed on Rolland Cascade New Life recycled paper.

For information about special discounts for bulk purchases, please contact Ingram Publisher Services at 1-800-961-7698.

ISBN: 1-933937-02-5

CONTENTS

ONE DAY WHITMAN insisted on holding [Horace]
Traubel's very cold hand when he arrived: "It is cold,
therefore I keep it. It is a reminiscence of the open air, the
sky, the sea, and no one knows how precious these are—
have been—to me. And indeed, it is to surcharge Leaves of
Grass with them that was my presiding spinal purpose
from the start."

—from Intimate with Walt: Selections from
Whitman's Conversations with Horace Traubel
1888-1892, edited by Gary Schmidgall

I believe whatever happens,
I shall not forget this earth...

—Walt Whitman

INTRODUCTION

Walt Whitman's nature poetry is unlike that of any other poet. Why
this is so is hard to say exactly, but the flow of his long lines, the
sharpness and sometimes quirkiness of his imagery, and his abundant
pleasure in being alive come together into an immediacy that really
does feel natural. It is art, of course, not a river or ocean waves. But
when he is at his best, he has a way of putting us into a natural place
with all its freshness. Poetry in the 19th Century favored a formal
approach and tone, and when Whitman came on the scene his work
struck some as dazzling, some as bewildering, and others as
outrageous. There were many reasons for this, but I think that each of
those reactions was due in part to a feeling in his readers that they
were having an experience in his poems that had more to do with
nature than literature. They were not used to poems being this fluid
and wet, or having so much open air.

Whitman's book, *Leaves of Grass*, was the work of decades. From
the age of thirty-seven on, he kept his title, adding new poems and
reorganizing and fine-tuning from edition to edition. The end-result
is a book as daunting as the Bible, to which Whitman compared it.
Approaching *Leaves of Grass* can be like trying to embrace a sequoia.
In focusing on his nature poetry, we won't get all of him, but we do
get a crucial part that is deeply connected to all that Whitman was
and wrote. We will also be reading some of his best, most living work.

While Whitman gave us some of the most vibrant nature poetry
we have, it should be acknowledged that he is also the author of one
of the most awful nature poems ever written. That would be "Song of
the Redwood-Tree," which combines a highly oratorical tone with a
dose of 19th Century boosterism of modern progress that is likely to
make 21st Century readers wince. In the poem Whitman accepts and
even celebrates the destruction of the big trees, as they make room for
"the flashing and golden pageant of California.../ Lands bathed in
sweeter, rarer, healthier air..." and for "a swarming and busy race
settling and organizing everywhere." Given the air pollution and
sprawl that have turned out to be so much a part of the pageant of

California, and of so many other places, the poem takes on a huge, sad irony. Whitman has the tree speak, encouraging its fellow redwoods to accept their fate: "With Nature's calm content, with tacit huge delight… For a superber race… For them we abdicate." The critic M. Jimmie Killingsworth in his recent book *Walt Whitman and the Earth* suggests that when Whitman wrote the poem he was depressed and on the verge of giving up, and that he projected this state of mind onto the redwood. True as this may be, it doesn't make the poem any easier to like.

There's always some unfairness in holding ancestors up to contemporary awareness. Still, there's a point to be made here beyond that Whitman's work is uneven. That is, he was not a conservationist. Whitman belonged to a time when the earth, even a single continent, still seemed nearly infinite to most people. Conservationists weren't very common in Whitman's time, but John Muir was only twenty years younger, and Thoreau was of his exact generation. Thoreau stood in opposition to his society's dominant values of business, expansion, and devotion to technology, and in solidarity with the natural world. Whitman, while he was political and capable of telling attacks on conventional society, was inside the social pulse in a way that Thoreau was not. He embraced the materialism and technology of his age. Thoreau's comments in *Walden* about the railroad are a classic meditation on the relative advantages and costs of technology and what is usually thought of as progress. Whitman, meanwhile, wrote an admiring and excited poem "To a Locomotive in Winter." Thoreau—even from childhood, according to relatives—was one to judge. Whitman was more accepting—of people, of the world in all its abundance and confusion.

Thoreau, the naturalist, the critic; Whitman, the celebrant, the democrat—different, yet with deep currents in common. What they had in common has been known as Transcendentalism, which included the beliefs that the physical world is also spiritual, and that human beings may yet become something more than we generally are. As they are two of the greatest embodiments of individualism that ever were, it's interesting to think of them together. They actually were together once, but no great conversation resulted. Thoreau, impressed with Whitman's poetry, went to Brooklyn to meet him. In Whitman's modest, working-class room, they sat and talked a little, but later when Thoreau's companion, Bronson Alcott, described the meeting, he said, "Each seemed planted fast in reserves, surveying the other curiously, like two beasts, each wondering what the other would do, whether to snap or run, and it came to no more than cold compliments between the two." Perhaps we can see in this brief encounter an early image of two kinds of environmentalist—the pure and the impure, the one that sees human beings as the problem and the one that sees them as part of nature—trying to figure out what to say to one another. It's a scenario that's been acted out in thousands of variations since then.

Years later, when Whitman visited Concord, he went to Thoreau's grave (and Hawthorne's, lying close by), and to Walden Pond. One of the homage stones in the cairn near the site of Thoreau's cabin was placed there by Whitman.

If Whitman wasn't a conservationist, what was he? We could call him an ecologist, if we consider the root meaning of the word, which is "house" or "home." Whitman wanted us to feel at home in our bodies and on the earth, and few writers match him in communicating that feeling. He himself was a robust, casual, observant human animal, with great warmth, sometimes expressed openly, sometimes held in as what he referred to as "subtle electric fire." Speaking of his work as a volunteer nurse and aid in army hospitals during the Civil War, Whitman said, "I fancy the reason I am able to do some good in the hospitals, among the poor languishing and wounded boys, is that I am so large and well—indeed like a great wild buffalo, with much hair—many of the soldiers are from the west, and far north—and they take to a man who has not the bleached shiny and shaved cut of the cities of the east." There was a kind of animal magnetism in Whitman that many felt and responded to—felt in his person, felt in his poetry. One woman, Anne Gilchrist, fell in love with him from reading his poetry and traveled from England hoping to marry him. Whitman, not much romantically inclined toward women, didn't encourage her, but she came. It didn't work out as she wished, but they became friends anyway.

In a number of places in his work Whitman expresses his admiration of animals and longs to be more like them. They seem to him solid, at one with themselves, "placid and self-contain'd." But it wasn't only animals in which he saw the vitality and aplomb he liked.

He saw the same qualities in certain human beings. Sometimes he saw many such people as he wandered around, looking with his sharp and luminous eyes. Look at some of the photographs of Whitman and you will see what I mean about his eyes. Reading his poems, the catalogues of images jotted one after another for instance, you can see that his eyes were sharp and luminous not only in their look but in their seeing as well.

As I was rereading *Leaves of Grass* to make this selection, I found it enjoyably difficult to know exactly what my definition of nature poetry should be. In "Give Me the Splendid Silent Sun," Whitman says that he enjoys the city at least as much as the country, human faces perhaps most of all. I decided on a liberal conception. Whitman liked the phrase "natural persons," and it could be that there is nothing more central to his vision than seeing human beings as every bit as natural as an oak-tree or a warbling bird. The presence of an oak, the singing of a mockingbird, the calm of cattle swishing their tails in the shade—these are things that he aspires to. The poems in this collection often catch the sense that humans and animals are an interesting continuum, that the terms "nature" and "nature writer" can't be limited by the categories of urban and rural, and that wilderness—the true, essential wilderness of the universe—is still with us as long as we can see a river or an ocean or the night sky.

I've mentioned Thoreau as a sort of complement to Whitman, and there's another of his contemporaries I'd like to mention as well. The 1850s were an amazing decade in American literature, and in American nature writing in particular, producing not only *Leaves of Grass* and *Walden*, but also *Moby Dick*. In a way, the story of Ahab is a sub-plot in the book's larger story, which is nature itself, contemplated through Melville's surrogate Ishmael, whose consciousness is one of the great intuitive, funny, poetic treasures of literature. When asked to make a list of outstanding works in the history of nature writing, Annie Dillard gave a one-sentence comment on *Moby Dick*: "The best book ever written about nature." Some readers find the chapters on whales and whaling overbearing and digressive, but to others they are the most wonderful part, where "the great flood-gates of the wonder-world [swing] open"—whales, the ocean, nature itself.

I bring in Melville because these three writers seem to belong together not only in the timing of their births and their greatest creative work, and not only as nature writers, but more particularly as water writers. Thoreau is the pond man par excellence, and the way he knows Walden Pond—its temperatures and depths, its fish and underwater sights, its boundaries and surrounding land, with limits at the same time it is infinite—is in keeping with the carefulness and clarity of his personality. Melville, on the other hand, is the ocean writer, the contemplator of whales and thousands of miles of water where there is no shore—and who knows where the bottom is? And Whitman? He is the writer of the places where water and land meet—seashore, creek and river bank, river-crossings on ferries, wading in surf, swims from beaches. Just as the pond expresses Thoreau's mind and the ocean Melville's, the water's edge expresses Whitman. In his poems we are very often in the place where we feel both the concrete immediacy of the here and now and the flux of time and eternity. On a ferry he leans on a solid rail stock-still, enjoying the sun and air, realizing at the same time that what is under and around him is all a flow.

There's no record that Whitman and Melville ever met, but it's possible that they saw each other. The opening chapter of *Moby Dick*, "Loomings," is one of the best essays ever written on the attraction of the human mind and soul to water. It is something instinctual, almost magical. Melville says, "Yes, as we all know, meditation and water are wedded forever." In this chapter he describes walking the shore of Manhattan on a Sunday afternoon and seeing multitudes of water-gazers, "posted like silent sentinels all around the town": "But look! here come more crowds, pacing straight for the water, and seemingly bound for a dive. Strange! Nothing will content them but the extremest limit of the land; loitering under the shady lee of yonder warehouses will not suffice. No. They must get just as nigh the water as they possibly can without falling in."

One of those water-gazers that Melville observed could well have been Whitman. He often wandered around Manhattan, and was drawn to the island's edges. He looked into the river and said, "Flood-tide below me! I see you face to face." On the other hand, if Whitman was one of the crowd heading for the water, he might not have stopped and stood transfixed in a reverie of water-contemplation. Just as likely, he would have been swimming, or watching the boys diving from the docks. In his days as a newspaperman, he wrote editorials praising the freedom and healthiness of such bathing, and he protested official attempts to prevent it. When he wasn't in Manhattan, Whitman often was out on the shore of Long Island (or Paumanok, as he liked to call it, using the Indian name), taking long bare-foot walks on the sand, or reciting Homer to the waves.

He loved to ramble on the seashore. As Killingsworth says, it was a sacred place for him, "most certainly the site of the soul's first on-set and deepest revelations...a site of survival, to which the poet returns again and again to reconnect with the earth and regenerate his energy." Whitman's poem describing the "on-set," "Out of the Cradle, Endlessly Rocking," is included here in its entirety. In it he unfolds a kind of poetry not possible in shorter lyrics. Besides describing the origin of his vocation as a poet, it demonstrates how Whitman was shaped by nature and by other influences as well. In "Out of the Cradle" he blends the seashore and a memory of an experience with a bird together with opera, another passion of his, and creates an extraordinary combination, a challenging poem which he said had to be read aloud to be understood.

"Out of the Cradle" addresses not only origins but death as well. At the end of the poem, in one of his most memorable passages, he hears death whispered in the water hissing into the sand, and he calls it "the low and delicious word," "rustling at my feet...laving me softly all over." D.H. Lawrence, one of Whitman's most caustic critics and eloquent advocates in one skin, thought he went too far in his attitude toward death—too much merging and union for Lawrence—and some psychological critics have suggested that there is something pathological in it. A statement like, "To die is different from what anyone supposed, and luckier," and a poem like "A Clear Midnight"—

> This is thy hour O Soul, thy free flight into the wordless,
> Away from books, away from art, the day erased, the lesson done,
> Thee fully forth emerging, silent, gazing, pondering the themes
>   thou lovest best,
> Night, sleep, death and the stars.

— can make Whitman seem a little too friendly with death.

Whatever else death is to Whitman, it is a part of nature. Whitman's attitude is not morbid; it is common sense raised to the level of poetry and wisdom. He mourns for dying and dead soldiers; he was hit hard by the death of his mother; at the death of a child he sat for hours silent, now and then thumping the floor hard with his cane. In "This Compost" he is "terrified at the earth, it is that calm and patient" as it accepts the leavings of death. But there is also, throughout his poetry, a pervasive realization that death is simply part of the earth's way of doing business. He knows that it is only with an awareness of death that we see life truly. Death is organic.

> *And as to you Corpse I think you are good manure, but that does*
> *   not offend me,*

> *I smell the white roses sweet-scented and growing,*
> *I reach to the leafy lips, I reach to the polish'd breasts of melons.*

It is an ending in one way, and a change in another.

> *And as to you Life I reckon you are the leavings of many deaths,*
> *(No doubt I have died myself ten thousand times before.)*

There is both release and grief in death.

> *Beautiful that war and all its deeds of carnage must in time be*
> *   utterly lost,*
> *That the hands of the sisters Death and Night incessantly softly*
> *wash again, and ever again, this soil'd world;*

He sensed something immortal in it: "The smallest sprout shows there is really no death." At one time he says, "I cannot answer the question of appearances or that of identity beyond the grave"; at other times he seems as sure about the individual soul's survival as a priest or minister at a funeral.

We disappear into the earth. It's a mystery. It's all right; don't panic, Whitman seems to say. There are many striking passages in Whitman's poetry about death, but if we had to choose one that gets to the heart of the matter, it might be these lines from the ending of "Song of Myself":

> *I bequeath myself to the dirt to grow from the grass I love,*
> *If you want me again look for me under your boot-soles.*

Not all of Whitman's nature poetry is in his poems. If we're open to a definition of poetry that includes prose—prose-poems, poetic prose—then there is a lot of poetry in Whitman's collection *Specimen Days*. Whether one wants to call it poetry or not, most of the best nature writing of Whitman's later life is in this book. Whitman's poetry tended to become more abstract and formal in its diction as he got older, but in his prose his sharpness of observation, casual tone, and flavorful phrasing stayed with him. (He maintained those qualities in his conversation too, as is clear in the comments recorded in the final years of his life by his friend Horace Traubel, recently edited by Gary Schmidgall as *Intimate with Walt*.) *Specimen Days* is very much a miscellany—"incongruous and full of skips and jumps," as Whitman says. He was fully aware of its randomness and roughness: "May-be, if I don't do anything else, I shall send out the most wayward, spontaneous, fragmentary book ever printed." It worked, and in this case a spontaneous and fragmentary approach produced many passages that feel like prose-poems—or we could just call them patches of poetic prose. They are a relaxed, here-and-now sort of poems. A more elaborate composition such as "Out of the Cradle" is clearly a performance, something magnificent, like opera. The prose excursions and observations of *Specimen Days* are casual, more like walks in the woods or letters from a friend.

Certain passages in *Specimen Days* give us our clearest sense that for Whitman nature was not only beautiful and mysterious but therapeutic as well. They were written when he was recovering from a series of strokes—brought on, he thought, as a result of his work in the war hospitals—that left him partly paralytic. Also during this time his mother died, which he described as "the saddest loss and sorrow of my life." He was at a low ebb, living mostly confined indoors at his brother's home in Camden, New Jersey. Relief and recovery came at a place twelve miles out in the country, Timber Creek (now Laurel Springs), where he found new friends and could again immerse himself in the natural world. In the woods along the creek he gave himself physical and spiritual therapy—sun-baths, mud-baths, nude strolls, wrestling with saplings, singing. He spoke of "the natural-medicinal, elemental-moral influences of the spot." He said that it may have saved his life.

Not all of *Specimen Days* is nature writing. It also includes reminiscences from early life, Civil War journals, reflections on literature, and more. But in the middle of the book, after giving a list of wildflowers he's observed, Whitman inserts this:

A CIVILITY TOO LONG NEGLECTED

The forgoing reminds me of something. As the individualities I would mainly portray have certainly been slighted by folks who make pictures, volumes, poems, out of them—as a faint testimonial of my own gratitude for many hours of peace and comfort in half-sickness, (and not by any means sure but they will somehow get wind of the compliment,) I hereby dedicate the last half of these SPECIMEN DAYS to the

bees,
black-birds,
dragon-flies,
pond-turtles,
mulleins, tansy, peppermint,
moths (great and little, some
*   splendid fellows,)*
glow-worms, (swarming millions
*   of them indescribably strange*
*   and beautiful at night over the*
*   pond and creek,)*

water-snakes,
crows,
millers,
mosquitoes,
butterflies,
wasps and hornets,
cat birds (and all other birds)
cedars,
tulip-trees (and all other trees),
and to the spots and memories of
those days, and of the creek.

Generally Whitman liked more space to work in than Basho and Issa, but he was their brother nonetheless in specificity, and in affection for ordinary creatures. There's a mixture of playfulness and reverence in him, and I think sometimes people get the reverence but miss the playfulness. Whitman's gesture of "civility" makes a beautiful dedication, and it would certainly serve for this book as well as for *Specimen Days*.

"Earth, my likeness" is a striking phrase. It seemed to me the right title for a selection of Whitman's nature poetry, yet it does raise the question of just what Whitman had in mind when he compared himself to the earth. Isn't that a pretty far-fetched comparison? The earth itself—rivers, oceans, mountains, forests, swamps, plains, deserts; the turning globe; implacable, inscrutable nature—where does Whitman get off claiming a resemblance to the earth? How accurate can the comparison be? Well, Whitman was audacious, and he enjoyed making large claims. In fact, comparing himself to the earth wasn't enough; he referred to himself as "a kosmos" as well.

The poem "Earth, My Likeness" comes from the Calamus group, Whitman's celebration of love between men. In that poem he senses in the earth "something fierce" that might "burst forth." He says that he and an athlete are in love with each other and that some comparable force might burst forth between them. That is the point of comparison here. This leads to another question—one that has been the subject of much debate: Other than poems, just what forms of expression did Whitman's affection and desire take? Gary Schmidgall's *A Gay Life* is one book that argues for Whitman's active homosexuality, and Jonathan Ned Katz's *Love Stories: Sex between Men before Homosexuality* presents a fascinating and nuanced examination of the subject.

That Whitman was gay in his feelings is pretty clear, though over the years many have denied or recast even that. We know that he wrote about men and his attraction to them a whole lot more, and a whole lot more urgently, than he did about women. We know he enjoyed putting his arm over a buddy's shoulders, and that he kissed men feelingly and slept with them. But in the 19th Century same-sex shows of affection and sleeping together were more commonplace, right? Did the penis—"this poem drooping shy and unseen that I always carry, and that all men carry...our lusty lurking masculine poems"—get involved? Besides the poems, Whitman left many clues and counter-clues about his love life, but we don't know the answer to that question for sure. Maybe that was the desire "eligible to burst forth" that he was feeling when he wrote "Earth, My Likeness."

However that may be, we have other testimony than Whitman's own that he did in fact resemble the earth. It comes from John Burroughs, who was Whitman's friend and became one of the best-known nature essayists of his time. He had been reading Whitman's poetry, and then met the man himself. Here is his description of their first meeting:

His book, read with modern eyes, would seem to justify Emerson's characterization of him as "half song thrush and half alligator;" and, by some means or other, I had got an impression that he was at least halfrowdy. Imagine my surprise, therefore, when I beheld a well-dressed, large, benevolent-looking man, cleanly and neat, with a griz-zly, shaggy appearance about the face and open throat.

Without rising he reached out to me a large, warm, soft hand, and regarded me with a look of infinite good nature and contentment. I was struck with the strange new beauty of him as he sat there in the gas light—the brightness of his eyes, the glow of his countenance, and the curious blending of youth and age in his expression. He was in that felicitous mood almost habitual to him, I have since found, during which his flesh and skin become, as it were, transparent, and allow his great summery, motherly soul to shine through.

Burroughs also wrote:

Notwithstanding the beauty and expressiveness of his eyes, I   occasionally see something in them as he bends them upon me, that almost makes me draw back. I cannot explain it—whether it is more, or less, than human. It is as if the earth looked at me—dumb, yearning, immodest, inhuman [unhuman?]. If the impersonal elements and forces were concentrated in an eye, that would be it.

In a letter to a friend, Burroughs said:

I have been much with Walt. Have even slept with him. I love him very much. The more I see and talk with him, the greater he becomes to me. He is as vast as the earth, and as loving and noble.

And three weeks later:

The more I see of Walt, the more I like him… He is far the wisest man I have ever met. There is nothing more to be said after he gives his views; it is as if Nature herself had spoken.

Burroughs was heterosexual—you might say a flaming heterosexual (though heterosexual, like homosexual, is our term, not the 19th Century's). His marriage was unhappy because of his wife's unresponsiveness to his sexual demands; he fathered his son with a local girl; the great love of his life was a woman he met when he was sixty-four and she was thirty-three. I won't try to unravel whatever sexual undercurrents there may be in Burroughs' feelings about Whitman; in fact, I'd rather leave them raveled. Sexuality is a great, flowing force. We don't have it so much as it has us. In that way it is like the earth, and the instinctual life that we share with the animals. Maybe what Burroughs was trying to say when he reached for earth images in describing what he felt in and for Whitman was this: He had met someone who seemed to him a force of nature.

Thinking back at the end of his life to Emerson's attempt to persuade him to take some of the sex out of *Leaves of Grass*, Whitman said, "if I had cut sex out I might just as well have cut everything out." The sex in his poetry is not located in just a few poems; it suffuses much more than an erotic or taboo poem here and there. When Whitman wrote about sex, he often wrote about it in terms of the natural world, and when he wrote about the natural world, he often wrote about it in terms of sexual intimacy and pleasure. The poems "Spontaneous Me" and "These I Singing in Spring" are perhaps the premier examples; no other walks in the woods in literature are quite like them. Eros and nature are richly tangled in a wet, lush bouquet. Whitman does not want us to separate them. The Jesuit poet Gerard Manley Hopkins probably comes closest to this effect, though his idea was that it is Christ and nature that are entangled. Hopkins said about Whitman, "I always knew in my heart Walt Whitman's mind to be more like my own than any other man's living. As he is a great scoundrel this is not a pleasant confession." Hopkins too recognized something wild, elemental, pre-Christian, in Whitman.

Whitman was a grateful guest of the earth. He was a model in that respect; one of the great praisers. He liked to be outdoors. He did much of his reading and writing there. He was a walker. He liked to recite poetry in the open air. He liked to loaf; his most famous description of a mystical experience begins, "Loaf with me on the grass...." He had a great capacity for enjoyment and amazement—sometimes in calm observation; sometimes as exuberance; sometimes as ecstasy. (And sometimes, besides these feelings and states of consciousness, there was despair as well.) Writing about sex as nature and nature as sex is more than a strategy or technique for Whitman. It is a measure of his happiness in being open to and in touch with the ground, the green world, animals, the water, the air, and the stars. His simple and brilliant title, *Leaves of Grass*, was just right for a book that grew so much out of the earth.

NOTE ON THE TEXT

The selections from *Specimen Days* are from the Dover Publications edition (1995). The poems are taken from *Leaves of Grass: Comprehensive Reader's Edition*, edited by Harold W. Blodgett and Sculley Bradley (New York University Press, 1965). Whitman was an inveterate reviser, sometimes for better, sometimes not. The textual variations are often fascinating, and those wanting to check them should see *Walt Whitman—Selected Poems 1855-1892*, edited by Gary Schmidgall (St. Martin's Press, 1999), which presents the poems in earlier versions. Whitman scholarship is a very active field, but the three works by Schmidgall cited in this Introduction represent an enormous outpouring of scholarly energy and intelligence and deserve to be singled out. The quotations from John Burroughs are taken from *Whitman in His Own Time*, edited by Joel Myerson (University of Iowa Press, 1991). *Walt Whitman: An Encyclopedia*, edited by J.R. LeMaster and Donald Kummings (Garland Publishing, 1998) is an especially useful critical source in that it is comprehensive and concise at the same time, a rich gathering of information and interpretation from Whitman scholars from across the country and the world.

I resisted the temptation to give titles to selections that are excerpts from longer works, but I suggest that they be read as poems which are something a little different from what they are in their original contexts, and which stand by themselves. I'll admit to having taken great pleasure in disassembling and rearranging what Walt Whitman so painstakingly assembled and arranged in *Leaves of Grass*. I hope he would be open to the project. Being in the company of his poems and the life they contain has been the deepest pleasure and nourishment. I am grateful to him every day.

Two Poems

THERE WAS A CHILD WENT FORTH

There was a child went forth every day,
And the first object he look'd upon, that object he became,
And that object became part of him for the day or a certain part of
    the day,
Or for many years or stretching cycles of years.

The early lilacs became part of this child,
And grass and white and red morning-glories, and white and red
    clover, and the song of the phoebe-bird,
And the Third-month lambs and the sow's pink-faint litter, and the
    mare's foal and the cow's calf,
And the noisy brood of the barnyard or by the mire of the pond-side,
And the fish suspending themselves so curiously below there, and the
    beautiful curious liquid,
And the water-plants with their graceful flat heads, all became part
    of him.

The field-sprouts of Fourth-month and Fifth-month became part
    of him,
Winter-grain sprouts and those of the light-yellow corn, and the
    esculent roots of the garden,
And the apple-trees cover'd with blossoms and the fruit afterward,
    and wood-berries, and the commonest weeds by the road,
And the old drunkard staggering home from the outhouse of the
    tavern whence he had lately risen,
And the schoolmistress that pass'd on her way to the school,
And the friendly boys that pass'd, and the quarrelsome boys,
And the tidy and fresh-cheek'd girls, and the barefoot negro boy
    and girl,
And all the changes of city and country wherever he went.

His own parents, he that had father'd him and she that had conceiv'd
    him in her womb and birth'd him,
They gave this child more of themselves than that,
They gave him afterward every day, they became part of him.

The mother at home quietly placing the dishes on the supper-table,
The mother with mild words, clean her cap and gown, a wholesome
    odor falling off her person and clothes as she walks by,
The father, strong, self-sufficient, manly, mean, anger'd, unjust,
The blow, the quick loud word, the tight bargain, the crafty lure,
The family usages, the language, the company, the furniture, the
    yearning and swelling heart,
Affection that will not be gainsay'd, the sense of what is real, he
    thought if after all it should prove unreal,
The doubts of day-time and the doubts of night-time, the curious
    whether and how,
Whether that which appears so is so, or is it all flashes and specks?
Men and women crowding fast in the streets, if they are not flashes
    and specks what are they?
The streets themselves and the facades of houses, and goods in the
    windows,
Vehicles, teams, the heavy-plank'd wharves, the huge crossing at
    the ferries,
The village on the highland seen from afar at sunset, the river between,
Shadows, aureola and mist, the light falling on roofs and gable of
    white or brown two miles off,
The schooner near by sleepily dropping down the tide, the little boat
    slack-tow'd astern,
The hurrying tumbling waves, quick-broken crests, slapping,
The strata of color'd clouds, the long bar of maroon-tint away
    solitary by itself, the spread of purity it lies motionless in,
The horizon's edge, the flying sea-crow, the fragrance of salt marsh
    and shore mud,
These became part of that child who went forth every day, and who
    now goes, and will always go forth every day.

THIS COMPOST

1

Something startles me where I thought I was safest,
I withdraw from the still woods I loved,
I will not go now on the pastures to walk,
I will not strip the clothes from my body to meet my lover the sea,
I will not touch my flesh to the earth as to other flesh to renew me.

O how can it be that the ground itself does not sicken?
How can you be alive you growths of spring?
How can you furnish health you blood of herbs, roots,
    orchards, grain?
Are they not continually putting distemper'd corpses within you?
Is not every continent worked over and over with sour dead?

Where have you disposed of their carcasses?
Those drunkards and gluttons of so many generations?
Where have you drawn off all the foul liquid and meat?
I do not see any of it upon you to-day, or perhaps I am deceived,
I will run a furrow with my plough, I will press my spade through
    the sod and turn it up underneath,
I am sure I shall expose some of the foul meat.

2

Behold this compost! behold it well!
Perhaps every mite has once form'd part of a sick person—
    yet behold!
The grass of spring covers the prairies,
The bean bursts noiselessly through the mould in the garden,
The delicate spear of the onion pierces upward,
The apple-buds cluster together on the apple-branches,
The resurrection of the wheat appears with pale visage out of
    its graves,
The tinge awakes over the willow-tree and the mulberry-tree,
The he-birds carol mornings and evenings while the she-birds sit
    on their nests,
The young of poultry break through the hatch'd eggs,

The new-born of animals appear, the calf is dropt from the cow,
the colt from the mare,
Out of its little hill faithfully rise the potato's dark green leaves,
Out of its hill rises the yellow maize-stalk, the lilacs bloom in
the dooryards,
The summer growth is innocent and disdainful above all those
strata of sour dead.

What chemistry!
That the winds are really not infectious,
That this is no cheat, this transparent green-wash of the sea
which is so amorous after me,
That it is safe to allow it to lick my naked body all over with its
tongues,
That it will not endanger me with the fevers that have deposited
themselves in it.
That all is clean forever and forever,
That the cool drink from the well tastes so good,
That blackberries are so flavorous and juicy,
That the fruits of the apple-orchard and the orange-orchard, that
melons, grapes, peaches, plums, will none of them poison me,
That when I recline on the grass I do not catch any disease,
Though probably every spear of grass rises out of what was once
a catching disease.

Now I am terrified at the Earth, it is that calm and patient,
It grows such sweet things out of such corruptions,
It turns harmless and stainless on its axis, with such endless
successions of diseas'd corpses,
It distills such exquisite winds out of such infused fetor,
It renews with such unwitting looks its prodigal, annual,
sumptuous crops,
It gives such divine materials to men, and accepts such leavings
from them at last.

Earthly Pleasures, Feeling Alive

From SONG OF MYSELF

The atmosphere is not a perfume, it has no taste of the distillation, it is
     odorless,
It is for my mouth forever, I am in love with it,
I will go to the bank by the wood and become undisguised and naked,
I am mad for it to be in contact with me.
The smoke of my own breath,
Echoes, ripples, buzz'd whispers, love-root, silk-thread, crotch and vine,
My respiration and inspiration, the beating of my heart, the passing of
     blood and air through my lungs,
The sniff of green leaves and dry leaves, and of the shore and dark-
     color'd sea-rocks, and of hay in the barn,
The sound of the belch'd words of my voice loos'd to the eddies of the
     wind,
A few light kisses, a few embraces, a reaching around of arms,
The play of shine and shade on the trees as the supple bows wag,
The delight alone or in the rush of the streets, or along the fields and
     hill-sides,
The feeling of health, the full-noon trill, the song of me rising from
     bed and meeting the sun.

From SONG OF MYSELF

I am he that walks with the tender and growing night,
I call to the earth and sea half-held by the night.

Press close bare-bosom'd night—press close magnetic
    nourishing night!
Night of south winds—night of the large few stars!
Still nodding night—mad naked summer night.

Smile O voluptuous cool-breath'd earth!
Earth of the slumbering and liquid trees!
Earth of departed sunset—earth of the mountains misty-top!
Earth of the vitreous pour of the full moon just tinged with blue!
Earth of shine and dark mottling the tide of the river!
Earth of the limpid gray of clouds brighter and clearer for my sake!
Far-swooping elbow'd earth—rich apple-blossom'd earth!
Smile, for your lover comes.

From SONG OF MYSELF

Divine am I inside and out, and I make holy whatever I touch
        or am touch'd from,
The scent of these arm-pits aroma finer than prayer,
This head more than churches, bibles, and all the creeds.

If I worship one thing more than another it shall be the spread
        of my own body, or any part of it,
Translucent mould of me it shall be you!
Shaded ledges and rests it shall be you!
Firm masculine colter it shall be you!
Whatever goes to the tilth of me it shall be you!
You my rich blood! your milky stream pale strippings of my life!
Breast that presses against other breasts it shall be you!
My brain it shall be your occult convolutions!
Root of wash'd sweet-flag! timorous pond-snipe!
        nest of guarded duplicate eggs! it shall be you!
Mix'd tussled hay of head, beard, brawn, it shall be you!
Trickling sap of maple, fibre of manly wheat, it shall be you!
Sun so generous it shall be you!
Vapors lighting and shading my face it shall be you!
You sweaty brooks and dews it shall be you!
Winds whose soft-tickling genitals rub against me it shall be you!
Broad muscular fields, branches of live oak, loving lounger
        in my winding paths, it shall be you!
Hands I have taken, face I have kiss'd, mortal I have ever touch'd,
        it shall be you.

ME IMPERTURBE

Me imperturbe, standing at ease in Nature,
Master of all or mistress of all, aplomb in the midst of irrational
things,
Imbued as they, passive, receptive, silent as they,
Finding my occupation, poverty, notoriety, foibles, crimes,
    less important than I thought,
Me toward the Mexican sea, or in the Mannahatta or the
Tennessee,
    or far north or inland,
A river man, or a man of the woods, or of any farm-life of these
States
    or of the coast, or the lakes or Kanada,
Me wherever my life is lived, O to be self-balanced for
contingencies,
To confront night, storms, hunger, ridicule, accidents, rebuffs,
    as the trees and animals do.

From SONG OF MYSELF

The big doors of the country barn stand open and ready,
The dried grass of the harvest-time loads the slow-drawn wagon,
The clear light plays on the brown gray and green intertinged,
The armfuls are pack'd to the sagging mow.

I am there, I help, I came stretch'd atop the load,
I felt its soft jolts, one leg reclined on the other,
I jump from the cross-beams and seize the clover and timothy,
And roll head over heels and tangle my hair full of wisps.

From A SONG OF JOYS

O boating on the rivers,
The voyage down the St. Lawrence, the superb scenery, the
steamers,
The ships sailing, the Thousand Islands, the occasional timber-
raft
    and the raftsmen with long-reaching sweep-oars,
The little huts on the rafts, and the steam of smoke
    when they cook supper at evening.

From SONG OF MYSELF

Upon a door-step, upon the horse-block of hard wood outside,
Upon the race-course, or enjoying picnics or jigs or a good game
    of baseball,
At he-festivals, with blackguard gibes, ironical license, bull-
    dances, drinking, laughter,
At the cider-mill tasting the sweets of the brown mash, sucking
    the juice through a straw,
At apple-peelings wanting kisses for all the red fruit I find,
At musters, beach-parties, friendly bees, huskings, house-raisings;
Where the mocking-bird sounds his delicious gurgles, cackles,
    screams, weeps,
Where the hay-rick stands in the barn-yard, where the dry-stalks
    are scatter'd, where the brood-cow waits in the hovel,
Where the bull advances to do his masculine work, where the
    stud to the mare, where the cock is treading the hen,
Where the heifers browse, where geese nip their food with short jerks,
Where the sun-down shadows lengthen over the limitless and
    lonesome prairie,
Where herds of buffalo make a crawling spread of the square
    miles far and near,
Where the humming-bird shimmers, where the neck of the long-
    lived swan is curving and winding,
Where the laughing-gull scoots by the shore, where she laughs
    her near-human laugh,
Where bee-hives range on a gray bench in the garden half hid
    by the high weeds,
Where band-neck'd partridges roost in a ring on the ground with
    their heads out,
Where burial coaches enter the arch'd gates of a cemetery,
Where winter wolves bark amid wastes of snow and icicled trees,
Where the yellow-crown'd heron comes to the edge of the marsh
    at night and feeds upon small crabs,
Where the splash of swimmers and divers cools the warm noon,
Where the katy-did works her chromatic reed on the walnut-tree
    over the well....

TO THE SPRING AND BROOK

So, still sauntering on, to the spring under the willows—musical as soft clinking glasses—pouring a sizeable stream, thick as my neck, pure and clear, out from its vent where the bank arches over like a great brown shaggy eyebrow or mouth-roof—gurgling, gurgling ceaselessly—meaning, saying something, of course (if one could only translate it)—always gurgling there, the whole year through—never giving out—oceans of mint, blackberries in summer—choice of light and shade—just the place for my July sun-baths and water-baths too—but mainly the inimitable soft sound-gurgles of it, as I sit there hot afternoons. How they and all grow into me, day after day—everything in keeping—the wild, just-palpable perfume, and the dapple of leaf-shadows, and all the natural-medicinal, elemental-moral influences of the spot.

A SUN-BATH—NAKEDNESS

Sunday, Aug. 27.—An hour or so after breakfast I wended my way down to the recesses of the aforesaid dell, which I and certain thrushes, cat-birds, &c., had all to ourselves. A light south-west wind was blowing through the tree-tops. It was just the place and time for my Adamic air-bath and flesh-brushing from head to foot. So hanging clothes on a rail near by, keeping old broadbrim straw on head and easy shoes on feet, haven't I had a good time the last two hours! First with the stiff elastic bristles rasping arms, breast, sides, till they turn'd scarlet—then partially bathing in the clear waters of the running brook—taking everything very leisurely, with many rests and pauses—stepping about barefooted every few minutes now and then in some neighboring black ooze, for unctuous mud-bath to my feet—a brief second and third rinsing in the crystal running waters—rubbing with the fragrant towel—slow negligent promenades on the turf up and down in the sun, varied with occasional rests, and further frictions of the bristle-brush—sometimes carrying my portable chair with me from place to place, as my range is quite extensive here, nearly a hundred rods, feeling quite secure from intrusion, (and that indeed I am not at all nervous about, if it accidentally happens.)

As I walk'd slowly over the grass, the sun shone out enough to show the shadow moving with me. Somehow I seem'd to get identity with each and every thing around me, in its condition. Nature was naked, and I was also.

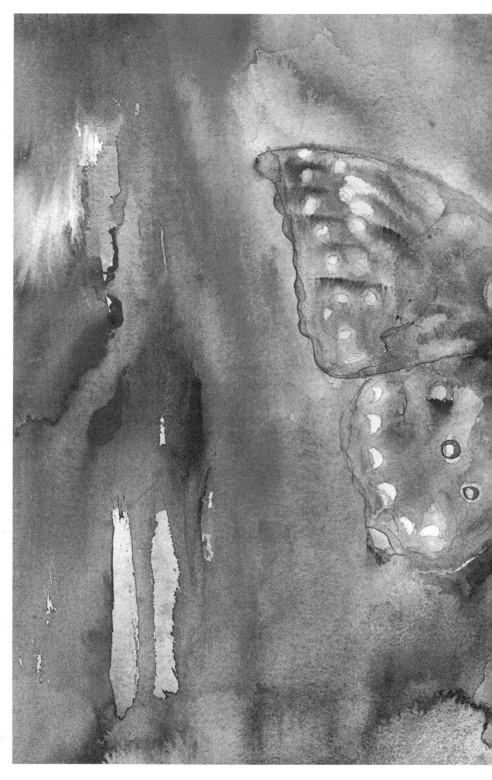

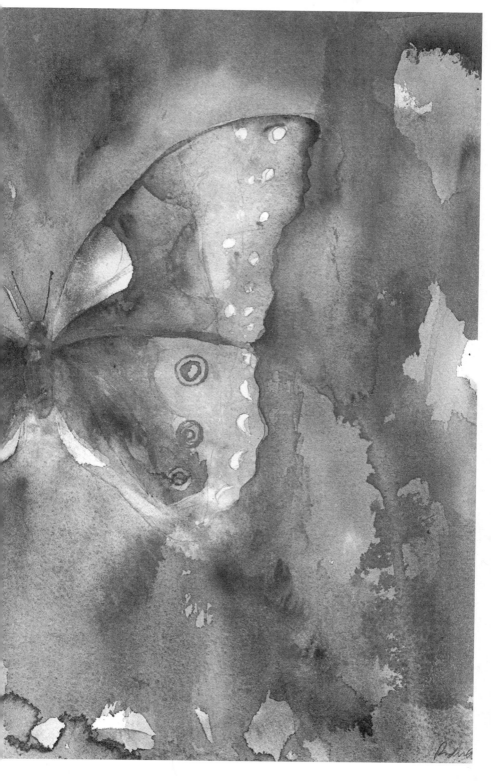

ANIMALS, BIRDS, AND INSECTS

From SONG OF MYSELF

I think I could turn and live with animals, they are so placid
     and self-contain'd,
I stand and look at them long and long.
They do not sweat and whine about their condition,
They do not lie awake in the dark and weep for their sins,
They do not make me sick discussing their duty to God,
Not one is dissatisfied, not one is demented with the mania
     of owning things,
Not one kneels to another, nor to his kind that lived thousands of
     years ago,
Not one is respectable or unhappy over the whole earth.

So they show their relations to me and I accept them,
They bring me tokens of myself, they evince them plainly
     in their possession.

I wonder where they get those tokens,
Did I pass that way huge times ago and negligently drop them?

From SONG OF MYSELF

As I have walk'd in Alabama my morning walk,
I have seen where the she-bird the mocking-bird sat on her
     nest in the briers hatching her brood.

I have seen the he-bird also,
I have paus'd to hear him near at hand inflating his throat
     and joyfully singing.

And while I paus'd it came to me that what he really sang for
     was not there only,
Nor for his mate nor himself only, nor all sent back by the echoes,
But subtle, clandestine, away beyond,
A charge transmitted and gift occult for those being born.

THE OX-TAMER

In a far-away northern country in the placid pastoral region,
Lives my farmer friend, the theme of my recitative,
    a famous tamer of oxen,
There they bring him the three-year-olds and the four-year-olds
    to break them,
He will take the wildest steer in the world and break him
    and tame him,
He will go fearless without any whip where the young bullock
    chafes up and down the yard,
The bullock's head tosses restless high in the air with raging eyes,
Yet see you! how soon his rage subsides—how soon
    this tamer tames him;
See you! on the farms hereabout a hundred oxen young and old,
    and he is the man who has tamed them,
They all know him, all are affectionate to him;
See you! some are such beautiful animals, so lofty looking;
Some are buff-color'd, some mottled, one has a white line
    running along his back, some are brindled,
Some have wide flaring horns (a good sign)—see you!
    the bright hides,
See, the two with stars on their foreheads—
    see, the round bodies and broad backs,
How straight and square they stand on their legs—
    what fine sagacious eyes!
How they watch their tamer—they wish him near them—
    how they turn and look after him!
What yearning expression! how uneasy they are when he
    moves away from them;
Now I marvel what it can be he appears to them,
    (books, politics, poems, depart—all else departs,)
I confess I envy only his fascination—my silent, illiterate friend,
Whom a hundred oxen love there in his life on farms,
In the northern country far, in the placid pastoral region.

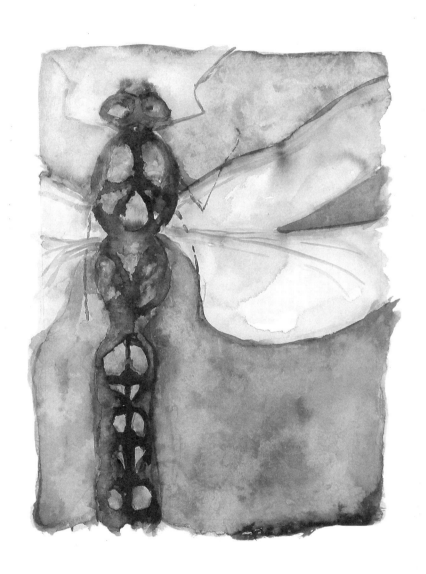

From SONG OF MYSELF

In me the caresser of life wherever moving, backward as well as
     forward sluing,
To niches aside and junior bending, not a person or object missing,
Absorbing all to myself and for this song.

Oxen that rattle the yoke and chain or halt in the leafy shade,
     what is that you express in your eyes?
It seems to me more than all the print I have read in my life.

My tread scares the wood-drake and wood-duck on my distant and
     day-long ramble,
They rise together, they slowly circle around.

I believe in those wing'd purposes,
And acknowledge red, yellow, white, playing within me,
And consider green and violet and the tufted crown intentional,
And do not call the tortoise unworthy because she is not something else,
And the jay in the woods never studied the gamut,
     yet trills pretty well to me,
And the look of the bay mare shames silliness out of me.

From BUMBLE-BEES

Nature marches in procession, in sections, like the corps of an army. All have done much for me, and still do. But for the last two days it has been the great wild bee, the humble-bee, or "bumble," as the children call him. As I walk, or hobble, from the farm-house down to the creek, I traverse the before-mention'd lane, fenced by old rails, with many splits, splinters, breaks, holes, &c., the choice habitat of those crooning, hairy insects. Up and down and by and between these rails, they swarm and dart and fly in countless myriads. As I wend slowly along, I am often accompanied with a moving cloud of them. They play a leading part in my morning, midday or sun-set rambles, and often dominate the landscape in a way I never before thought of—fill the long lane, not by scores or hundreds only, but by thousands. Large and vivacious and swift, with wonderful momentum and a loud swelling perpetual hum, varied now and then with something almost like a shriek, they dart to and fro, in rapid flashes, chasing each other, and (little things as they are,) conveying to me a new and pronounc'd sense of strength, beauty, vitality and movement. Are they in their mating season? or what is the meaning of this plenitude, swiftness, eagerness, display? As I walk'd, I thought I was followed by a particular swarm, but upon observation I saw that it was a rapid succession of changing swarms, one after another.

As I write, I am seated under a big wild-cherry tree—the warm day temper'd by partial clouds and a fresh breeze, neither too heavy nor light—and here I sit long and long, envelop'd in the deep musical drone of these bees, flitting, balancing, darting to and fro about me by hundreds—big fellows with light yellow jackets, great glistening swelling bodies, stumpy heads and gauzy wings—humming their perpetual rich mellow boom. (Is there not a hint in it for a musical composition, of which it should be the back-ground? some bumble-bee symphony?) How it all nourishes, lulls me, in the way most needed; the open air, the rye-fields, the apple orchards. The last two days have been faultless in sun, breeze, temperature and everything; never two more perfect days, and I have enjoy'd them wonderfully. My health is somewhat better, and my spirit at peace. (Yet the anniversary of the saddest loss and sorrow of my life is close at hand.)

Another jotting, another perfect day: forenoon, from 7 to 9, two hours envelop'd in sound of bumble-bees and bird-music. Down in the apple-trees and in a neighboring cedar were three or four russet-back'd thrushes, each singing his best; and roulading in ways I never heard surpass'd. Two hours I abandon myself to hearing them, and indolently absorbing the scene. Almost every bird I notice has a special time in the year— sometimes limited to a few days—when it sings its best; and now is the period of these russet-backs. Meanwhile, up and down the lane, the darting, droning, musical bumble-bees. A great swarm again for my entourage as I return home, moving along with me as before.

SUNDOWN PERFUME—QUAIL-NOTES—THE HERMIT THRUSH

June 19th, 4 to 6^1/$_2$ P.M.—Sitting alone by the creek—solitude here, but the scene bright and vivid enough—the sun shining, and quite a fresh wind blowing (some heavy showers last night,) the grass and trees looking their best—the clare-obscure of different greens, shadows, half-shadows, and the dappling glimpses of water, through recesses—the wild flageolet-note of a quail nearby—the just-heard fretting of some hylas down there in the pond—crows cawing in the distance—a drove of young hogs rooting in soft ground near the oak near which I sit—some come sniffing near me, and then scamper away with grunts. And still the clear notes of the quail—the quiver of leave-shadows over the paper as I write—the sky aloft, with white clouds, and the sun well declining to the west—the swift darting of many sand-swallows coming and going, their holes in a neighboring marl-bank—the odor of the cedar and oak, so palpable, as evening approaches—perfume, color, the bronze-and-gold of nearly ripen'd wheat—clover-fields, with honey-scent—the well-up maize, with long and rustling leaves—the great patches of thriving potatoes, dusky green, fleck'd all over with white blossoms—the old, warty, venerable oak above me—and ever, mix'd with the dual tones of the quail, the soughing of the wind through some near-by pines.

As I rise for return, I linger long to a delicious song-epilogue (is it the hermit-thrush?) from some bushy recess off there in the swamp, repeated leisurely and pensively over and over again. This, to the circle-gambols of the swallows flying by dozens in concentric rings in the last rays of sunset, like flashes of some airy wheel.

From HUDSON RIVER SIGHTS

But there is one sight the very grandest. Sometimes in the fiercest driving storm of wind, rain, hail or snow, a great eagle will appear over the river, now soaring with steady and now overhended wings—always confronting the gale, or perhaps cleaving into, or at times literally *sitting* upon it. It is like reading some first-class natural tragedy or epic, or hearing martial trumpets. The splendid bird enjoys the hubbub—is adjusted and equal to it—finishes it so artistically. His pinions just oscillating—the position of his head and neck—his resistless, occasionally varied flight—now a swirl, now an upward movement—the black clouds driving—the angry wash below—the hiss of rain, the wind's piping (perhaps the ice colliding, grunting)—he tacking or jibing—now, as it were, for a change, abandoning himself to the gale, moving with it with such velocity—and now, resuming control, he comes up against it, lord of the situation and the storm—lord, amid it, of power and savage joy.

THE DALLIANCE OF EAGLES

Skirting the river road, (my forenoon walk, my rest,)
Skyward in air a sudden muffled sound, the dalliance of eagles,
The rushing amorous contact high in space together,
The clinching interlocking claws, a living, fierce, gyrating wheel,
Four beating wings, two beaks, a swirling mass tight grappling,
In tumbling turning clustering loops, straight downward falling,
Till o'er the river pois'd, the twain yet one, a moment's lull,
A motionless still balance in the air, then parting, talons loosing,
Upward again on slow-firm pinions slanting, their separate
     diverse flight,
She hers, he his, pursuing.

AN UNKNOWN

June 15.—To-day I noticed a new large bird, size of a nearly grown hen—a haughty, white-bodied dark-wing'd hawk—I suppose a hawk from his bill and general look—only he had a clear, loud, quite musical, sort of bell-like call, which he repeated again and again, at intervals, from a lofty dead tree-top, over-hanging the water. Sat there a long time, and I on the opposite bank watching him. Then he darted down, skimming pretty close to the stream—rose slowly, a magnificent sight, and sail'd with steady wide-spread wings, no flapping at all, up and down the pond two or three times, near me, in circles in clear sight, as if for my delectation. Once he came quite close over my head; I saw plainly his hook'd bill and hard restless eyes.

LOCUSTS AND KATYDIDS.

Aug. 22.—Reedy monotones of locusts, or sounds of katydid—I hear the latter at night, and the other both day and night. I thought the morning and evening warble of birds delightful; but I find I can listen to these strange insects with just as much pleasure. A single locust is now heard near noon from a tree two hundred feet off, as I write—a long, whirring, continued, quite loud noise graded in distinct whirls, or swinging circles, increasing in strength and rapidity up to a certain point, and then a fluttering, quietly tapering fall. Each strain is continued from one to two minutes. The locust-song is very appropriate to the scene—gushes, has meaning, is masculine, is like some fine old wine, not sweet, but far better than sweet.

But the katydid—how shall I describe its piquant utterances? One sings from a willow-tree just outside my open bedroom window, twenty yards distant; every clear night for a fortnight past has sooth'd me to sleep. I rode through a piece of woods for a hundred rods the other evening, and heard the katydids by myriads—very curious for once; but I like better my single neighbor on the tree.

A NOISELESS PATIENT SPIDER

A noiseless patient spider,
I mark'd where on a little promontory it stood isolated,
Mark'd how to explore the vacant vast surrounding,
It launch'd forth filament, filament, filament, out of itself,
Ever unreeling them, ever tirelessly speeding them.

And you O my soul where you stand,
Surrounded, detached, in measureless oceans of space,
Ceaselessly musing, venturing, throwing, seeking the spheres
        to connect them,
Till the bridge you will need be form'd, till the ductile anchor hold,
Till the gossamer thread you fling catch somewhere, O my soul.

MIRACLES

MIRACLES

Why, who makes much of a miracle?
As to me I know of nothing else but miracles,
Whether I walk the streets of Manhattan,
Or dart my sight over the roofs of houses toward the sky,
Or wade with naked feet along the beach just in the edge of
the water,
Or stand under trees in the woods,
Or talk by day with any one I love, or sleep in the bed at night
        with any one I love,
Or sit at table at dinner with the rest,
Or look at strangers opposite me riding in the car,
Or watch honey-bees busy around the hive of a summer forenoon,
Or animals feeding in the fields,
Or birds, or the wonderfulness of insects in the air,
Or the wonderfulness of the sundown, or of stars shining so
        quiet and bright,
Or the exquisite delicate thin curve of the new moon in spring,
These with the rest, one and all, are to me miracles,
The whole referring, yet each distinct and in its place.

To me every hour of the light and dark is a miracle,
Every cubic inch of space is a miracle,
Every square yard of the surface of the earth is spread with the same,
Every foot of the interior swarms with the same.

To me the sea is a continual miracle,
The fishes that swim—the rocks—the motion of the waves—
        the ships with men in them,
What stranger miracles are there?

From SONG OF MYSELF

I believe a leaf of grass is no less than the journey-work of the stars,
And the pismire is equally perfect, and a grain of sand, and the
      egg of the wren,
And the tree-toad is a chef-d'oeuvre for the highest,
And the running blackberry would adorn the parlors of heaven,
And the narrowest hinge in my hand puts to scorn all machinery,
And the cow crunching with depress'd head surpasses any statue,
And a mouse is miracle enough to stagger sextillions of infidels.

UNTIL YOU CAN EXPLAIN

Priests!
Until you can explain a paving stone, do not try to explain God:
Until your creeds can do as much as apples and hen's eggs, let
      down your eyebrows a little,
Until your Bibles and prayer-books are able to walk like me,
And until your brick and mortar can procreate as I can,
I beg you, Sirs, do not presume to put them above me.

ORANGE BUDS BY MAIL FROM FLORIDA

[*Voltaire closed a famous argument by claiming that a ship of war and the grand opera were proofs enough of civilization's and France's progress, in his day.*]

A lesser proof than old Voltaire's, yet greater,
Proof of this present time, and thee, thy broad expanse, America,
To my plain Northern hut, in outside clouds and snow,
Brought safely for a thousand miles o'er land and tide,
Some three days since on their own soil live-sprouting,
Now here their sweetness through my room unfolding,
A bunch of orange buds by mail from Florida.

THOUGHTS UNDER AN OAK—A DREAM

June 2.—This is the fourth day of a dark northeast storm, wind and rain. Day before yesterday was my birthday. I have now enter'd on my 60th year. Every day of the storm, protected by overshoes and a waterproof blanket, I regularly come down to the pond, and ensconce myself under the lee of the great oak; I am here now writing these lines. The dark smoke-color'd clouds roll in furious silence athwart the sky; the soft green leaves dangle all round me; the wind steadily keeps up its hoarse, soothing music over my head—Nature's mighty whisper. Seated here in solitude I have been musing over my life—connecting events, dates, as links of a chain, neither sadly nor cheerily, but somehow, to-day here under the oak, in the rain, in an unusually matter-of-fact spirit.

But my great oak—sturdy, vital, green—five feet thick at the butt. I sit a great deal near or under him. Then the tulip tree near by—the Apollo of the woods—tall and graceful, yet robust and sinewy, inimitable in hang of foliage and throwing-out of limb; as if the beauteous, vital, leafy creature could walk, if it only would. (I had a sort of dream-trance the other day, in which I saw my favorite trees step out and promenade up, down and around, very curiously—with a whisper from one, leaning down as he pass'd me. We do all this on the present occasion, exceptionally, just for you.)

THE LESSON OF A TREE

Sept. 1.—I should not take either the biggest or the most picturesque tree to illustrate it. Here is one of my favorites now before me, a fine yellow poplar, quite straight, perhaps 90 feet high, and four thick at the butt. How strong, vital, enduring! how dumbly eloquent! What suggestions of imperturbability and being, as against the human trait of mere seeming. Then the qualities, almost emotional, palpably artistic, heroic, of a tree; so innocent and harmless, yet so savage. It is, yet says nothing. How it rebukes by its tough and equable serenity all weathers, this gusty-temper'd little whiffet, man, that runs indoors at a mite of rain or snow. Science (or rather half-way science) scoffs at reminiscence of dryad and hamadryad, and of trees speaking. But, if they don't, they do as well as most speaking, writing, poetry, sermons—or rather they do a great deal better. I should say indeed that those old dryad-reminiscences are quite as true as any, and profounder than most reminiscences we get. ("Cut this out," as the quack mediciners say, and keep by you.) Go and sit in a grove or woods, with one or more of those voiceless companions, and read the foregoing, and think.

From DEBRIS

I will take an egg out of the robin's nest in the orchard,
I will take a branch of gooseberries from the old bush in the
        garden, and go and preach to the world;
You shall see I will not meet a single heretic or scorner,
You shall see how I stump clergymen, and confound them,
You shall see me showing a scarlet tomato, and a white pebble
        from the beach.

From SONG OF MYSELF

And as to you Death, and you bitter hug of mortality, it is idle to
    try to alarm me.

To his work without flinching the accoucheur comes,
I see the elder-hand pressing receiving supporting,
I recline by the sills of the exquisite flexible doors,
And mark the outlet, and mark the relief and escape.

And as to you Corpse I think you are good manure, but that does
    not offend me,
I smell the white roses sweet-scented and growing,
I reach to the leafy lips, I reach to the polish'd breasts of melons.

And as to you Life I reckon you are the leavings of many deaths,
(No doubt I have died myself ten thousand times before.)

From SONG OF MYSELF

A child said *What is the grass?* fetching it to me with full hands;
How could I answer the child? I do not know what it is
    any more than he.

I guess it must be the flag of my disposition,
    out of hopeful green stuff woven.

Or I guess it is the handkerchief of the Lord,
A scented gift and remembrancer designedly dropt,
Bearing the owner's name someway in the corners, that we may
    see and remark, and say *Whose?*

Or I guess the grass is itself a child, the produced babe of the
vegetation.

Or I guess it is a uniform hieroglyphic,
And it means, Sprouting alike in broad zones and narrow zones,
Growing among black folks as among white,
Kanuck, Tuckahoe, Congressman, Cuff, I give them the same,
      I receive them the same.

And now it seems to me the beautiful uncut hair of graves.

Tenderly will I use you curling grass,
It may be you transpire from the breasts of young men,
It may be if I had known them I would have loved them,
It may be you are from old people, or from offspring taken soon
      out of their mother's laps,
And here you are the mother's laps.

This grass is very dark to be from the white heads of old mothers,
Darker than the colorless beards of old men,
Dark to come from under the faint red roofs of mouths.

O I perceive after all so many uttering tongues,
And I perceive they do not come from the roofs of
      mouths for nothing.

I wish I could translate the hints about the dead young men
      and women,
And the hints about old men and mothers, and the offspring
      taken soon out of their laps.
What do you think has become of the young and old men?
And what do you think has become of the women and children?

They are alive and well somewhere,
The smallest sprout shows there is really no death,
And if ever there was it led forward life, and does not wait at the
      end to arrest it,
And ceas'd the moment life appear'd.

All goes onward and outward, nothing collapses,
And to die is different from what any one supposed, and luckier.

From I SING THE BODY ELECTRIC

O my body! I dare not desert the likes of you in other men and
women, nor the likes of the parts of you,
I believe the likes of you are to stand or fall with the likes of the
soul, (and that they are the soul,)
I believe the likes of you are to stand or fall with my poems, and
that they are my poems,
Man's, woman's, child's, youth's, wife's, husband's, mother's,
father's, young man's, young woman's poems,
Head, neck, hair, ears, drop and tympan of the ears,
Eyes, eye-fringes, iris of the eye, eyebrows, and the waking or
sleeping of the lids,
Mouth, tongue, lips, teeth, roof of mouth, jaws, and the jaw-hinges,
Nose, nostrils of the nose, and the partition,
Cheeks, temples, forehead, chin, throat, back of the neck, neck-slue,
Strong shoulders, manly beard, scapula, hind-shoulders, and the
ample side-round of the chest,
Upper-arm, armpit, elbow-socket, lower-arm, arm-sinews,
arm-bones,
Wrist and wrist-joints, hand, palm, knuckles, thumb, forefinger,
finger-joints, finger-nails,
Broad breast-front, curling hair of the breast, breast-bone,
breast-side,
Ribs, belly, backbone, joints of the backbone,
Hips, hip-sockets, hip-strength, inward and outward round, man-
balls, man-root,
Strong set of thighs, well carrying the trunk above,
Leg-fibres, knee, knee-pan, upper-leg, under-leg,
Ankles, instep, foot-ball, toes, toe-joints, the heel;
All attitudes, all the shapeliness, all the belongings of my or your
body or any one's body, male or female,
The lung-sponges, the stomach-sac, the bowels sweet and clean,
The brain in its folds inside the skull-frame,
Sympathies, heart-valves, palate-valves, sexuality, maternity,
Womanhood, and all that is a woman, and the man that comes
from woman,

The womb, the teats, nipples, breast-milk, tears, laughter,
　　weeping, love-looks, love-perturbations and risings,
The voice, articulation, language, whispering, shouting aloud,
Food, drink, pulse, digestion, sweat, sleep, walking, swimming,
Poise on the hips, leaping, reclining, embracing, arm-curving and
　　tightening,
The continual changes of the flex of the mouth,
　　and around the eyes,
The skin, the sunburnt shade, freckles, hair,
The curious sympathy one feels when feeling with the hand the
　　naked meat of the body,
The circling rivers the breath, and breathing it in and out,
The beauty of the waist, and thence of the hips, and thence
　　downward toward the knees,
The thin red jellies within you or within me, the bones and the
　　marrow in the bones,
The exquisite realization of health;
O I say these are not the parts and poems of the body only, but
　　of the soul,
O I say now these are the soul!

From SONG OF MYSELF

Do you guess I have some intricate purpose?
Well I have, for the Fourth-month showers have, and the mica on
    the side of a rock has.

Do you take it I would astonish?
Does the daylight astonish? does the early redstart twittering
    through the woods?
Do I astonish more than they?

This hour I tell things in confidence,
I might not tell everybody, but I will tell you.

NATURAL PERSONS

GIVE ME THE SPLENDID SILENT SUN

1

Give me the splendid silent sun with all his beams full-dazzling,
Give me juicy autumnal fruit ripe and red from the orchard,
Give me a field where the unmow'd grass grows,
Give me an arbor, give me the trellis'd grape,
Give me fresh corn and wheat, give me serene-moving animals
     teaching content,
Give me nights perfectly quiet as on high plateaus west of the
     Mississippi, and I looking up at the stars,
Give me odorous at sunrise the garden of beautiful flowers
     where I can walk undisturb'd,
Give me for marriage a sweet-breath'd woman of whom I should
     never tire,
Give me a perfect child, give me away aside from the noise of
     the world a rural domestic life,
Give me to warble spontaneous songs recluse by myself, for my
     own ears only,
Give me solitude, give me Nature, give me again O Nature your
     primal sanities!

These demanding to have them, (tired with ceaseless excitement,
     and rack'd by the war-strife,)
These to procure incessantly asking, rising in cries from my heart,
While yet incessantly asking still I adhere to my city,
Day upon day and year upon year O city, walking your streets,
Where you hold me enchain'd a certain time refusing to give me up,
Yet giving to make me glutted, enrich'd of soul, you give me
     forever faces;
(O I see what I sought to escape, confronting, reversing my cries,
I see my own soul trampling down what it ask'd for.)

2

Keep your splendid silent sun,
Keep your woods O Nature, and the quiet places by the woods,
Keep your fields of clover and timothy, and your corn-fields and
    orchards,
Keep the blossoming buckwheat fields where the Ninth-month
    bees hum,
Give me faces and streets—give me these phantoms incessant
    and endless along the trottoirs!
Give me interminable eyes—give me women—give me comrades
    and lovers by the thousand!
Let me see new ones every day—let me hold new ones by the
    hand every day!
Give me such shows—give me the streets of Manhattan!
Give me Broadway, with the soldiers marching—give me the
    sound of the trumpets and drums!
(The soldiers in companies or regiments—some starting away,
    flush'd and reckless,
Some, their time up, returning with thinn'd ranks, young, yet
    very old, worn, marching, noticing nothing;)
Give me the shores and wharves heavy-fringed with black ships!
O such for me! O an intense life, full to repletion and varied!
The life of the theatre, bar-room, huge hotel, for me!
The saloon of the steamer! the crowded excursion for me! the
    torchlight procession!
The dense brigade bound for the war, with high piled military
    wagons following;
People, endless, streaming, with strong voices, passions, pageants,
Manhattan streets with their powerful throbs, with beating drums
    as now,
The endless and noisy chorus, the rustle and clank of muskets,
    (even the sight of the wounded,)
Manhattan crowds, with their turbulent musical chorus!
Manhattan faces and eyes forever for me.

From A SONG OF JOYS

O to have been brought up on bays, lagoons, creeks, or along
    the coast,
To continue and be employ'd there all my life,
The briny and damp smell, the shore, the salt weeds exposed at
    low water,
The work of fishermen, the work of the eel-fisher and clam-fisher;
I come with my clam-rake and spade, I come with my eel-spear,
Is the tide out? I join the group of clam-diggers on the flats,
I laugh and work with them, I joke at my work like a mettlesome
    young man;
In winter I take my eel-basket and eel-spear and travel out on
    foot on the ice—I have a small axe to cut holes in the ice,
Behold me well-clothed going gayly or returning in the afternoon,
    my brood of tough boys accompanying me,
My brood of grown and part-grown boys, who love to be with no
    one else so well as they love to be with me,
By day to work with me, and by night to sleep with me.

From OUR OLD FEUILLAGE

The camp of Georgia wagoners just after dark, the supper-fires
    and the cooking and eating by whites and negroes,
Thirty or forty great wagons, the mules, cattle, horses, feeding
    from troughs,
The shadows, gleams, up under the leaves of the old sycamore-
    trees, the flames with the black smoke from the pitch-pine
    curling and rising....

From SONG OF MYSELF

The boatmen and clam-diggers arose early and stopt for me,
I tuck'd my trowser-ends in my boots and went and had a good time;
You should have been with us that day round the chowder-kettle.

From SONG OF MYSELF

The negro holds firmly the reins of his four horses, the block
      swags underneath on its tied-over chain,
The negro that drives the long dray of the stone-yard, steady and
      tall he stands pois'd on one leg on the string-piece,
His blue shirt exposes his ample neck and breast and loosens over
      his hip-band,
His glance is calm and commanding, he tosses the slouch of his
      hat away from his forehead,
The sun falls on his crispy hair and mustache, falls on the black
      of his polish'd and perfect limbs.

From THE SLEEPERS

Now what my mother told me one day as we sat at dinner
    together,
Of when she was a nearly grown girl living with her parents on
    the old homestead.

A red squaw came one breakfast-time to the old homestead,
On her back she carried a bundle of rushes for rush-bottoming
    chairs,
Her hair, straight, shiny, coarse, black, profuse, half-envelop'd her
    face,
Her step was free and elastic, and her voice sounded exquisitely
    as she spoke.

My mother look'd in delight and amazement at the stranger,
She look'd at the freshness of her tall-borne face and full and
    pliant limbs,
The more she look'd upon her she loved her,
Never before had she seen such wonderful beauty and purity,
She made her sit on a bench by the jamb of the fireplace, she
    cook'd food for her,
She had no work to give her, but she gave her remembrance and
    fondness.

The red squaw staid all the forenoon, and toward the middle of
    the afternoon she went away,
O my mother was loth to have her go away,
All the week she thought of her, she watch'd for her many a
    month,
She remember'd her many a winter and many a summer,
But the red squaw never came nor was heard of there again.

THE RUNNER

On a flat road runs the well-train'd runner,
He is lean and sinewy with muscular legs,
He is thinly clothed, he leans forward as he runs,
With lightly closed fists and arms partially rais'd.

BEAUTIFUL WOMEN

Women sit or move to and fro, some old, some young,
The young are beautiful—but the old are more beautiful
     than the young.

From I SING THE BODY ELECTRIC

I knew a man, a common farmer, the father of five sons,
And in them the fathers of sons, and in them the fathers of sons.

This man was of wonderful vigor, calmness, beauty of person,
The shape of his head, the pale yellow and white of his hair and
    beard, the immeasurable meaning of his black eyes, the
    richness and breadth of his manners,
These I used to go and visit him to see, he was wise also,
He was six feet tall, he was over eighty years old, his sons were
    massive, clean, bearded, tan-faced, handsome,
They and his daughters loved him, all who saw him loved him,
They did not love him by allowance, they loved him with
    personal love,
He drank water only, the blood show'd like scarlet through the
    clear-brown skin of his face,
He was a frequent gunner and fisher, he sail'd his boat himself,
    he had a fine one presented him by a ship-joiner, he had
    fowling pieces presented to him by men that loved him,
When he went with his five sons and many grand-sons to hunt or
    fish, you would pick him out as the most beautiful and
    vigorous of the gang,
You would wish long and long to be with him, you would wish to
    sit by him in the boat that you might touch each other.

From SONG OF MYSELF

Twenty-eight young men bathe by the shore,
Twenty-eight young men and all so friendly;
Twenty-eight years of womanly life and all so lonesome.

She owns the fine house by the rise of the bank,
She hides handsome and richly drest aft the blinds of the
window.

Which of the young men does she like the best?
Ah the homeliest of them is beautiful to her.

Where are you off to, lady? for I see you,
You splash in the water there, yet stay stock still in your room.

Dancing and laughing along the beach came the twenty-ninth bather,
The rest did not see her, but she saw them and loved them.

The beards of the young men glisten'd with wet, it ran from their
        long hair,
Little streams pass'd all over their bodies.

An unseen hand also pass'd over their bodies,
It descended tremblingly from their temples and ribs.

The young men float on their backs, their white bellies bulge to
        the sun, they do not ask who seizes fast to them,
They do not know who puffs and declines with pendant and
        bending arch,
They do not think whom they souse with spray.

From A SONG FOR OCCUPATIONS

When the psalm sings instead of the singer,
When the script preaches instead of the preacher,
When the pulpit descends and goes instead of the carver that
    carved the supporting desk,
When I can touch the body of books by night or by day, and
    when they touch my body back again,
When a university course convinces like a slumbering woman
    and child convince,
When the minted gold in the vault smiles like the night-
    watchman's daughter,
When warrantee deeds loafe in chairs opposite and are my
    friendly companions,
I intend to reach them my hand, and make as much of them as I
    do of men and women like you.

THE SEA

OUT OF THE CRADLE ENDLESSLY ROCKING

Out of the cradle endlessly rocking,
Out of the mocking-bird's throat, the musical shuttle,
Out of the Ninth-month midnight,
Over the sterile sands and the fields beyond, where the child
     leaving his bed wander'd alone, bareheaded, barefoot,
Down from the shower'd halo,
Up from the mystic play of shadows twining and twisting as if
     they were alive,
Out from the patches of briers and blackberries,
From the memories of the bird that chanted to me,
From your memories sad brother, from the fitful risings and
     fallings I heard,
From under that yellow half-moon late-risen and swollen as if
     with tears,
From those beginning notes of yearning and love there in the mist,
From the thousand responses of my heart never to cease,
From the myriad thence-arous'd words,
From the word stronger and more delicious than any,
From such as now they start the scene revisiting,
As a flock, twittering, rising, or overhead passing,
Borne hither, ere all eludes me, hurriedly,
A man, yet by these tears a little boy again,
Throwing myself on the sand, confronting the waves,
I, chanter of pains and joys, uniter of here and hereafter,
Taking all hints to use them, but swiftly leaping beyond them,
A reminiscence sing.

Once Paumanok,
When the lilac-scent was in the air and Fifth-month grass was
     growing,
Up this seashore in some briers,
Two feather'd guests from Alabama, two together,
And their nest, and four light-green eggs spotted with brown,
And every day the he-bird to and fro near at hand,
And every day the she-bird crouch'd on her nest,
     silent, with bright eyes,   .

And every day I, a curious boy, never too close, never
    disturbing them,
Cautiously peering, absorbing, translating.

Shine! shine! shine!
Pour down your warmth, great sun!
While we bask, we two together.

Two together!
Winds blow south, or winds blow north,
Day come white, or night come black,
Home, or rivers and mountains from home,
Singing all time, minding no time,
While we two keep together.

Till of a sudden,
May-be kill'd, unknown to her mate,
One forenoon the she-bird crouch'd not on the nest,
Nor return'd that afternoon, nor the next,
Nor ever appear'd again.

And thenceforward all summer in the sound of the sea,
And at night under the full moon in calmer weather,
Over the hoarse surging of the sea,
Or flitting from brier to brier by day,
I saw, I heard at intervals the remaining one, the he-bird,
The solitary guest from Alabama.

Blow! blow! blow!
Blow up sea-winds along Paumanok's shore;
I wait and I wait till you blow my mate to me.

Yes, when the stars glisten'd,
All night long on the prong of a moss-scallop'd stake,
Down almost amid the slapping waves,
Sat the lone singer wonderful causing tears.

He call'd on his mate,
He pour'd forth the meanings which I of all men know.

Yes my brother I know,
The rest might not, but I have treasur'd every note,
For more than once dimly down to the beach gliding,
Silent, avoiding the moonbeams, blending myself with the
    shadows,
Recalling now the obscure shapes, the echoes, the sounds and
    sights after their sorts,
The white arms out in the breakers tirelessly tossing,
I, with bare feet, a child, the wind wafting my hair,
Listen'd long and long.

Listen'd to keep, to sing, now translating the notes,
Following you my brother.

Soothe! soothe! soothe!
Close on its waves soothes the wave behind,
And again another behind embracing and lapping, every one close,
But my love soothes not me, not me.

Low hangs the moon, it rose late,
It is lagging—O I think it is heavy with love, with love.

O madly the sea pushes upon the land,
With love, with love.

O night! do I not see my love fluttering out among the breakers?
What is that little black thing I see there in the white?

Loud! loud! loud!
Loud I call to you, my love!

High and clear I shoot my voice over the waves,
Surely you must know who is here, is here,
You must know who I am, my love.

Low-hanging moon!
What is that dusky spot in your brown yellow?
O it is the shape, the shape of my mate!
O moon do not keep her from me any longer.

Land! land! O land!
Whichever way I turn, O I think you could give me my mate back again if
*   you only would,*
For I am almost sure I see her dimly whichever way I look.

O rising stars!
Perhaps the one I want so much will rise, will rise with some of you.

O throat! O trembling throat!
Sound clearer through the atmosphere!
Pierce the woods, the earth,
Somewhere listening to catch you must be the one I want.

Shake out carols!
Solitary here, the night's carols!
Carols under the lagging, yellow, waning moon!
O under the moon where she droops almost down into the sea!
O reckless despairing carols.

But soft! sink low!
Soft! let me just murmur,
And do you wait a moment you husky-nois'd sea,
For somewhere I believe I heard my mate responding to me,
So faint, I must be still, be still to listen,
But not altogether still, for then she might not come immediately to me.

Hither my love!
Here I am! here!
With this just-sustain'd note I announce myself to you,
This gentle call is for you my love, for you.

Do not be decoy'd elsewhere,
That is the whistle of the wind, it is not my voice,
That is the fluttering, the fluttering of the spray,
Those are the shadows of leaves.

O darkness! O in vain!
O I am very sick and sorrowful.

O brown halo in the sky near the moon, drooping upon the sea!
O troubled reflection in the sea!
O throat! O throbbing heart!
And I singing uselessly, uselessly all the night.

O past! O happy life! O songs of joy!
In the air, in the woods, over fields,
Loved! loved! loved! loved! loved!
But my mate no more, no more with me!
We two together no more.

The aria sinking,
All else continuing, the stars shining,
The winds blowing, the notes of the bird continuous echoing,
With angry moans the fierce old mother incessantly moaning,
On the sands of Paumanok's shore gray and rustling,
The yellow half-moon enlarged, sagging down, drooping, the face
    of the sea almost touching,
The boy ecstatic, with his bare feet the waves, with his hair the
    atmosphere dallying,
The love in the heart long pent, now loose, now at last
    tumultuously bursting,
The aria's meaning, the ears, the soul, swiftly depositing,
The strange tears down the cheeks coursing,
The colloquy there, the trio, each uttering,
The undertone, the savage old mother incessantly crying,
To the boy's soul's questions sullenly timing, some drown'd secret
    hissing,

To the outsetting bard.
Demon or bird! (said the boy's soul,)
Is it indeed toward your mate you sing? or is it really to me?
For I, that was a child, my tongue's use sleeping, now I have
      heard you,
Now in a moment I know what I am for, I awake,
And already a thousand singers, a thousand songs, clearer, louder
      and more sorrowful than yours,
A thousand warbling echoes have started to life within me, never
      to die.

O you singer solitary, singing by yourself, projecting me,
O solitary me listening, never more shall I cease perpetuating you,
Never more shall I escape, never more the reverberations,
Never more the cries of unsatisfied love be absent from me,
Never again leave me to be the peaceful child I was before what
      there in the night,
By the sea under the yellow and sagging moon,
The messenger there arous'd, the fire, the sweet hell within,
The unknown want, the destiny of me.

O give me the clew! (it lurks in the night here somewhere,)
O if I am to have so much, let me have more!

A word then, (for I will conquer it,)
The word final, superior to all,
Subtle, sent up—what is it?—I listen;
Are you whispering it, and have been all the time, you sea-waves?
Is that it from your liquid rims and wet sands?

Whereto answering, the sea,
Delaying not, hurrying not,
Whisper'd me through the night, and very plainly before day-break,
Lisp'd to me the low and delicious word death,
And again death, death, death, death,
Hissing melodious, neither like the bird nor like my arous'd
      child's heart,

But edging near as privately for me rustling at my feet,
Creeping thence steadily up to my ears and laving me softly all
      over,
Death, death, death, death, death.

Which I do not forget,
But fuse the song of my dusky demon and brother,
That he sang to me in the moonlight on Paumanok's gray beach,
With the thousand responsive songs at random,
My own songs awaked from that hour,
And with them the key, the word up from the waves,
The word of the sweetest song and all songs,
That strong and delicious word which, creeping to my feet,
(Or like some old crone rocking the cradle, swathed in sweet
      garments, bending aside,)
The sea whisper'd me.

From PAUMANOK, AND MY LIFE ON IT AS CHILD AND YOUNG MAN

But many a good day or half-day did I have, wandering through those solitary cross-roads, inhaling the peculiar and wild aroma. Here, and all along the island and its shores, I spent intervals many years, all seasons, sometimes riding, sometimes boating, but generally afoot, (I was always then a good walker,) absorbing fields, shores, marine incidents, characters, the bay-men, farmers, pilots—always had a plentiful acquaintance with the latter, and with fishermen—went every summer on sailing trips—always liked the bare sea-beach, south side, and have some of my happiest hours on it to this day.

As I write, the whole experience comes back to me after the lapse of forty or more years—the soothing rustle of the waves, and the saline smell—boyhood's times, the clam-digging, bare-foot, and with trowsers roll'd up—hauling down the creek— the perfume of the sedge meadows—the hay-boat, and the chowder and fishing excursions;--or, of later years, little voyages down and out New York bay, in the pilot boats. Those same later years, also, while living in Brooklyn, (1836-'50) I went regularly every week in the mild seasons down to Coney island, at that time a long, bare unfrequented shore, which I had all to myself, and where I loved, after bathing, to race up and down the hard sand, and declaim Homer or Shakspere to the surf and sea-gulls by the hour.

From SONG OF MYSELF

You sea! I resign myself to you also—I guess what you mean,
I behold from the beach your crooked inviting fingers,
I believe you refuse to go back without feeling of me,
We must have a turn together, I undress, hurry me out of sight
    of the land,
Cushion me soft, rock me in billowy drowse,
Dash me with amorous wet, I can repay you.

From THE SLEEPERS

The beach is cut by the razory ice-wind, the wreck-guns sound,
The tempest lulls, the moon comes floundering through the drifts.

I look where the ship helplessly heads end on, I hear the burst as
    she strikes, I hear the howls of dismay, they grow fainter
    and fainter.

I cannot aid with my wringing fingers,
I can but rush to the surf and let it drench me and freeze upon me.

I search with the crowd, not one of the company is wash'd to
    us alive,
In the morning I help pick up the dead and lay them in rows
    in a barn.

From AS I EBB'D WITH THE OCEAN OF LIFE

As I wend to the shores I know not,
As I list to the dirge, the voices of men and women wreck'd,
As I inhale the impalpable breezes that set in upon me,
As the ocean so mysterious rolls toward me closer and closer,
I too but signify at the utmost a little wash'd up drift,
A few sands and dead leaves to gather,
Gather, and merge myself as part of the sands and drift.

O baffled, balk'd to the very earth,
Oppress'd with myself that I have dared to open my mouth,
Aware now that amid all that blab whose echoes recoil upon me
      I have not once had the least idea who or what I am,
But that before all my arrogant poems the real Me stands yet
      untouch'd, untold, altogether unreach'd,
Withdrawn far, mocking me with mock-congratulatory signs
      and bows,
With peals of distant ironical laughter at every word I have written,
Pointing in silence to these songs, and then to the sand beneath.

I perceive I have not really understood any thing, not a single
      object, and that no man ever can,
Nature here in sight of the sea taking advantage of me to dart
      upon me and sting me,
Because I have dared to open my mouth to sing at all.

THE WORLD BELOW THE BRINE

The world below the brine,
Forests at the bottom of the sea, the branches and leaves,
Sea-lettuce, vast lichens, strange flowers and seeds, the thick
    tangle, openings, and pink turf,
Different colors, pale gray and green, purple, white, and gold,
    the play of light through the water,
Dumb swimmers there among the rocks, coral, gluten, grass,
    rushes, and the aliment of the swimmers,
Sluggish existences grazing there suspended, or slowly crawling
    close to the bottom,
The sperm-whale at the surface blowing air and spray, or
    disporting with his flukes,
The leaden-eyed shark, the walrus, the turtle, the hairy sea-
    leopard, and the sting-ray,
Passions there, wars, pursuits, tribes, sight in those ocean-depths,
    breathing that thick-breathing air, as so many do,
The change thence to the sight here, and to the subtle air
    breathed by beings like us who walk this sphere,
The change onward from ours to that of beings who walk other
    spheres.

A PAUMANOK PICTURE

Two boats with nets lying off the sea-beach, quite still,
Ten fishermen waiting—they discover a thick school of
      mossbonkers—they drop the join'd seine-ends in the water,
The boats separate and row off, each on its rounding course to
      the beach, enclosing the mossbonkers,
The net is drawn in by a windlass by those who stop ashore,
Some of the fishermen lounge in their boats, others stand ankle-
      deep in the water, pois'd on strong legs,
The boats partly drawn up, the water slapping against them,
Strew'd on the sand in heaps and windrows, well out from the
      water, the green-back'd spotted mossbunkers.

HAD I THE CHOICE

Had I the choice to tally greatest bards,
To limn their portraits, stately, beautiful, and emulate at will,
Homer with all his wars and warriors—Hector, Achilles, Ajax,
Or Shakspere's woe-entangled Hamlet, Lear, Othello—
      Tennyson's fair ladies,
Metre or wit the best, or choice conceit to wield in perfect
      rhyme, delight of singers;
These, these, O sea, all these I'd gladly barter,
Would you the undulation of one wave, its trick to me transfer,
Or breathe one breath of yours upon my verse,
And leave its odor there.

Herbage and Comrades

THESE I SINGING IN SPRING

These I singing in spring collect for lovers,
(For who but I should understand lovers and all their sorrow and joy?
And who but I should be the poet of comrades?)
Collecting I traverse the garden of the world, but soon I pass the gates,
Now along the pond-side, now wading in a little, fearing not the wet,
Now by the post-and-rail fences where the old stones thrown
        there, pick'd from the fields, have accumulated,
(Wild-flowers and vines and weeds come up through the stones
        and partly cover them, beyond these I pass,)
Far, far in the forest, or sauntering later in the summer, before I
        think where I go,
Solitary, smelling the earthy smell, stopping now and then in the
        silence,
Alone I had thought, yet soon a troop gathers around me,
Some walk by my side and some behind, and some embrace my
        arms or neck,
They the spirits of dear friends dead or alive, thicker they come,
        a great crowd, and I in the middle,
Collecting, dispensing, singing, there I wander with them,
Plucking something for tokens, tossing toward whoever is near me,
Here, lilac, with a branch of pine,
Here, out of my pocket, some moss which I pull'd off a live-oak
        in Florida as it hung trailing down,
Here, some pinks and laurel leaves, and a handful of sage,
And here what I now draw from the water, wading in the pond-side,
(O here I last saw him that tenderly loves me, and returns again
        never to separate from me,
And this, O this shall henceforth be the token of comrades, this
        calamus-root shall,
Interchange it youths with each other! let none render it back!)
And twigs of maple and a bunch of wild orange and chestnut,
And stems of currants and plum-blows, and the aromatic cedar,
These I compass'd around by a thick cloud of spirits,
Wandering, point to or touch as I pass, or throw them loosely
        from me,
Indicating to each one what he shall have, giving something to each;
But what I drew from the water by the pond-side, that I reserve,
I will give of it, but only to them that love as I myself am capable
        of loving.

92

I SAW IN LOUISIANA A LIVE-OAK GROWING

I saw in Louisiana a live-oak growing,
All alone stood it and the moss hung down from the branches,
Without any companion it grew there uttering joyous leaves of
    dark green,
And its look, rude, unbending, lusty, made me think of myself,
But I wonder'd how it could utter joyous leaves standing alone
    there without its friend near, for I knew I could not,
And I broke off a twig with a certain number of leaves upon it,
    and twined around it a little moss,
And brought it away, and I have placed it in sight in my room,
It is not needed to remind me as of my own dear friends,
(For I believe lately I think of little else than of them,)
Yet it remains to me a curious token, it makes me think of
    manly love;
For all that, and though the live-oak glistens there in Louisiana
    solitary in a wide flat space,
Uttering joyous leaves all its life without a friend a lover near,
I know very well I could not.

EARTH, MY LIKENESS

Earth, my likeness,
Though you look so impassive, ample and spheric there,
I now suspect that is not all;
I now suspect there is something fierce in you
      eligible to burst forth,
For an athlete is enamor'd of me, and I of him,
But toward him there is something fierce and terrible in me
      eligible to burst forth,
I dare not tell it in words, not even in these songs.

MULLEINS AND MULLEINS

Large, placid mulleins, as summer advances, velvety in
texture, of a light greenish-drab color, growing everywhere in
the fields—at first earth's big rosettes in their broad-leav'd low
cluster-plants, eight, ten, twenty leaves to a plant—plentiful
on the fallow twenty-acre lot, at the end of the lane, and
especially by the ridge-sides of the fences—then close to the
ground, but soon springing up—leaves as broad as my hand,
and the lower ones twice as long—so fresh and dewy in the
morning—stalks now four or five, even seven or eight feet
high. The farmers, I find, think the mullein a mean unworthy
weed, but I have grown to a fondness for it. Every object has
its lesson, enclosing the suggestion of everything else—and
lately I sometimes think all is concentrated for me in these
hardy, yellow-flower'd weeds. As I come down the lane early
in the morning, I pause before their soft wool-like fleece and
stem and broad leaves, glittering with countless diamonds.
Annually for three summers now, they and I have silently
return'd together; at such long intervals I stand or sit among
them, musing—and woven with the rest, of so many hours
and moods of partial rehabilitation—of my sane or sick spirit,
here as near at peace as it can be.

THE OAKS AND I

Sept. 5, '77.—I write this, 11 A.M., shelter'd under a dense oak by the bank, where I have taken refuge from a sudden rain. I came down here, (we had sulky drizzles all the morning, but an hour ago a lull,) for the before-mention'd daily and simple exercise I am fond of—to pull on that young hickory sapling out there—to sway and yield to its tough-limber upright stem—haply to get into my old sinews some of its elastic fibre and clear sap. I stand on the turf and take these health-pulls moderately and at intervals for nearly an hour, inhaling great draughts of fresh air. Wandering by the creek, I have three or four naturally favorable spots where I rest—besides a chair I lug with me and use for more deliberate occasions. At other spots convenient I have selected, besides the hickory just named, strong and limber boughs of beech or holly, in easy-reaching distance, for my natural gymnasia, for arms, chest, trunk-muscles. I can soon feel the sap and sinew rising through me, like mercury to heat. I hold on boughs or slender trees caressingly there in the sun and shade, wrestle with their innocent stalwartness—and know the virtue thereof passes from them into me. (Or may-be we interchange—may-be the trees are more aware of it all than I ever thought.)

Aug. 4, 6 P.M.—Lights and shades and rare effects on tree-foliage and grass—transparent greens, grays, &c., all in sunset pomp and dazzle. The clear beams are now thrown in many new places, on the quilted, seam'd, bronze-drab, lower tree-trunks, shadow'd except at this hour—now flooding their young and columnar ruggedness with strong light, unfolding to my sense new amazing features of silent, shaggy charm, the solid bark, the expression of harmless impassiveness, with many a bulge and gnarl unreck'd before. In the revealings of such light, such exceptional hour, such mood, one does not wonder at the old story fables, (indeed, why fables?) of people falling into love-sickness with trees, seiz'd extatic with the mystic realism of the resistless silent strength in them—strength, which after all is perhaps the last, completest, highest beauty.

ROOTS AND LEAVES THEMSELVES ALONE

Roots and leaves themselves alone are these,
Scents brought to me and women from the wild woods and
      pond-side,
Breast-sorrel and pinks of love, fingers that wind around tighter
      than vines,
Gushes from the throats of birds hid in the foliage of trees as the
      sun is risen,
Breezes of land and love set from living shores to you on the
      living sea, to you O sailors!
Frost-mellow'd berries and Third-month twigs offer'd fresh to
      young persons wandering out in the fields when the winter
      breaks up,
Love-buds put before you and within you whoever you are,
Buds to be unfolded on the old terms,
If you bring the warmth of the sun to them they will open and
      bring form, color, perfume, to you,
If you become the aliment and the wet they will become flowers,
      fruits, tall branches and trees.

From SONG OF MYSELF

Loafe with me on the grass, loose the stop from your throat,
Not words, not music or rhyme I want, nor custom or lecture,
    not even the best,
Only the lull I like, the hum of your valved voice.

I mind how once we lay such a transparent summer morning,
How you settled your head athwart my hips and gently turn'd
    over upon me,
And parted the shirt from my bosom-bone, and plunged your
    tongue to my bare-stript heart,
And reach'd till you felt my beard, and reach'd till you held my
    feet.

Swiftly arose and spread around me the peace and knowledge
    that pass all the argument of the earth,
And I know that the hand of God is the promise of my own,
And I know that the spirit of God is the brother of my own,
And that all the men ever born are also my brothers, and the
    women my sisters and lovers,
And that a kelson of the creation is love,
And limitless are leaves stiff or drooping in the fields,
And brown ants in the little wells beneath them,
And mossy scabs of the worm fence, heap'd stones, elder,
    mullein, and poke-weed.

SPONTANEOUS ME

Spontaneous me, Nature,
The loving day, the mounting sun, the friend I am happy with,
The arm of my friend hanging idly over my shoulder,
The hillside whiten'd with blossoms of the mountain ash,
The same late in autumn, the hues of red, yellow, drab, purple,
    and light and dark green,
The rich coverlet of the grass, animals and birds, the private
    untrimm'd bank, the primitive apples, the pebble-stones,
Beautiful dripping fragments, the negligent list of one after
    another as I happen to call them to me or think of them,
The real poems, (what we call poems being merely pictures,)
The poems of the privacy of the night, and of men like me,
This poem drooping shy and unseen that I always carry, and that
    all men carry,
(Know once for all, avow'd on purpose, wherever are men like
    me, are our lusty lurking masculine poems,)
Love-thoughts, love-juice, love-odor, love-yielding, love-climbers,
    and the climbing sap,
Arms and hands of love, lips of love, phallic thumb of love,
    breasts of love, bellies press'd and glued together with love,
Earth of chaste love, the body of the woman I love, the body of
    the man, the body of the earth,
Soft forenoon airs that blow from the south-west,
The hairy wild-bee that murmurs and hankers up and down,
    that gripes the full-grown lady-flower, curves upon her with
    amorous firm legs, takes his will of her, and holds himself
    tremulous and tight till he is satisfied;
The wet of woods through the early hours,
Two sleepers at night lying close together as they sleep, one with
    an arm slanting down across and below the waist of the
    other,
The smell of apples, aromas from crush'd sage-plant, mint,
    birch-bark,
The boy's longings, the glow and pressure as he confides to me
    what he was dreaming,
The dead leaf whirling its spiral whirl and falling still and
    content to the ground,
The no-form'd stings that sights, people, objects, sting me with,

The hubb'd sting of myself, stinging me as much as it ever can
	any one,
The sensitive, orbic, underlapp'd brothers, that only privileged
	feelers may be intimate where they are,
The curious roamer the hand roaming all over the body, the
	bashful withdrawing of flesh where the fingers soothingly
	pause and edge themselves,
The limpid liquid within the young man,
The vex'd corrosion so pensive and so painful,
The torment, the irritable tide that will not be at rest,
The like of the same I feel, the like of the same in others,
The young man that flushes and flushes, and the young woman
	that flushes and flushes,
The young man that wakes deep at night, the hot hand seeking
	to repress what would master him,
The mystic amorous night, the strange half-welcome pangs,
	visions, sweats,
The pulse pounding through palms and trembling encircling
	fingers, the young man all color'd, red, ashamed, angry;
The souse upon me of my lover the sea, as I lie willing and
	naked,
The merriment of the twin babes that crawl over the grass in the
	sun, the mother never turning her vigilant eyes from them,
The walnut-trunk, the walnut-husks, and the ripening or ripen'd
	long-round walnuts,
The continence of vegetables, birds, animals,
The consequent meanness of me should I skulk or find myself
	indecent, while birds and animals never once skulk or find
	themselves indecent,
The great chastity of paternity, to match the great chastity of
	maternity,
The oath of procreation I have sworn, my Adamic and fresh
	daughters,
The greed that eats me day and night with hungry gnaw, till I
	saturate what shall produce boys to fill my place when I
	am through,
The wholesome relief, repose, content,
And this bunch pluck'd at random from myself,
It has done its work—I toss it carelessly to fall where it may.

MOMENTS

ONE OF THE HUMAN KINKS

How is it that in all the serenity and lonesomeness of solitude, away off here amid the hush of the forest, alone, or as I have found in prairie wilds, or mountain stillness, one is never entirely without the instinct of looking around, (I never am, and others tell me the same of themselves, confidentially,) for somebody to appear, or start up out of the earth, or from behind some tree or rock? Is it a lingering, inherited remains of man's primitive wariness, from the wild animals? or from his savage ancestry far back? It is not at all nervousness or fear. Seems as if something unknown were possibly lurking in those bushes, or solitary places. Nay, it is quite certain there is—some vital unseen presence.

A NIGHT REMEMBRANCE

Aug. 25, 9–10 A.M.—I sit by the edge of the pond, everything quiet, the broad polish'd surface spread before me—the blue of the heavens and the white clouds reflected from it—and flitting across, now and then, the reflection of some flying bird. Last night I was down here with a friend till after midnight; everything a miracle of splendor—the glory of the stars, and the completely rounded moon—the passing clouds, silver and luminous-tawny—now and then masses of vapory illuminated scud—and silently by my side my dear friend. The shades of the trees, the patches of moonlight on the grass—the softly blowing breeze, and just-palpable odor of the neighboring ripening corn—the indolent and spiritual night, inexpressibly rich, tender, suggestive—something altogether to filter through one's soul, and nourish and feed and soothe the memory long afterwards.

THE TORCH

On my Northwest coast in the midst of the night a fisherman's
      group stands watching,
Out on the lake that expands before them, others are
      spearing salmon,
The canoe, a dim shadowy thing, moves across the black water,
Bearing a torch ablaze at the prow.

A FARM PICTURE

Through the ample open door of the peaceful country barn,
A sunlit pasture field with cattle and horses feeding,
And haze and vista, and the far horizon fading away.

AN ULSTER COUNTY WATERFALL

I jot this mem. in a wild scene of woods and hills, where we have
come to visit a waterfall. I never saw finer or more copious
hemlocks, many of them large, some old and hoary. Such a
sentiment to them, secretive, shaggy—what I call weather-beaten
and let-alone—a rich underlay of ferns, yew sprouts and mosses,
beginning to be spotted with the early summer wild-flowers.
Enveloping all, the monotone and liquid gurgle from the hoarse
impetuous copious fall—the greenish-tawny, darkly transparent
waters, plunging with velocity down the rocks, with patches of
milk-white foam—a stream of hurrying amber, thirty feet wide,
risen far back in the hills and woods, now rushing with volume—
every hundred rods a fall, and sometimes three or four in that
distance. A primitive forest, druidical, solitary and savage—not
ten visitors a year—broken rocks everywhere—shade overhead,
thick underfoot with leaves—a just palpable wild and delicate
aroma.

From CROSSING BROOKLYN FERRY

It avails not, time nor place—distance avails not,
I am with you, you men and women of a generation, or ever so
    many generations hence,
Just as you feel when you look on the river and sky, so I felt,
Just as any of you is one of a living crowd, I was one of a crowd,
Just as you are refresh'd by the gladness of the river and the
    bright flow, I was refresh'd,
Just as you stand and lean on the rail, yet hurry with the swift
    current, I stood yet was hurried,
Just as you look on the numberless masts of ships and the thick-
    stemm'd pipes of the steamboats, I look'd.

I too many and many a time cross'd the river of old,
Watched the Twelfth-month sea-gulls, saw them high in the air
    floating with motionless wings, oscillating their bodies,
Saw how the glistening yellow lit up parts of their bodies and left
    the rest in strong shadow,
Saw the reflection of the summer sky in the water,
Had my eyes dazzled by the shimmering track of beams,
Look'd at the fine centrifugal spokes of light round the shape of
    my head in the sunlit water....

From OUR OLD FEUILLAGE

Evening—me in my room—the setting sun,
The setting summer sun shining in my open window, showing the
      swarm of flies, suspended, balancing in the air in the
      centre of the room, darting athwart, up and down,
      casting swift shadows in specks on the opposite wall
      where the shine is....

From SONG OF MYSELF

Logic and sermons never convince,
The damp of the night drives deeper into my soul....

TO THE SUN-SET BREEZE

Ah, whispering, something again, unseen,
Where late this heated day thou enterest at my window, door,
Thou, laving, tempering all, cool-refreshing, gently vitalizing
Me, old, alone, sick, weak-down, melted-worn with sweat;
Thou, nestling, folding close and firm yet soft, companion better
      than talk, book, art,
(Thou hast, O Nature! elements! utterance to my heart beyond
      the rest—and this is of them,)
So sweet thy primitive taste to breathe within—thy soothing
      fingers on my face and hands,
Thou, messenger-magical strange bringer to body and spirit of me,
(Distances balk'd—occult medicines penetrating me
      from head to foot,)
I feel the sky, the prairies vast—I feel the mighty northern lakes,
I feel the ocean and the forest—somehow I feel the globe itself
      swift-swimming in space;
Thou blown from lips so loved, now gone—haply from the
      endless store, God-sent,
(For thou art spiritual, Godly, most of all known to my sense,)
Minister to speak to me, here and now, what word has never told,
      and cannot tell,
Art thou not universal concrete's distillation? Law's, all
      Astronomy's last refinement?
Hast thou no soul? Can I not know, identify thee?

NIGHT SKYS

WHEN I HEARD THE LEARN'D ASTRONOMER

When I heard the learn'd astronomer,
When the proofs, the figures, were ranged in columns before me,
When I was shown the charts and diagrams, to add, divide, and
    measure them,
When I sitting heard the astronomer where he lectured with
    much applause in the lecture-room,
How soon unaccountable I became tired and sick,
Till rising and gliding out I wander'd off by myself,
In the mystical moist night-air, and from time to time,
Look'd up in perfect silence at the stars.

THE MOON

May 18.—I went to bed early last night, but found myself waked
shortly after 12, and, turning awhile sleepless and mentally
feverish, I rose, dress'd myself, sallied forth and walk'd down the
lane. The full moon, some three or four hours up—a sprinkle of
light and less-light clouds just lazily moving—Jupiter an hour
high in the east, and here and there throughout the heavens a
random star appearing and disappearing. So, beautifully veil'd
and varied—the air, with that early-summer perfume, not at all
damp or raw—at times Luna languidly emerging in richest
brightness for minutes, and then partially envelop'd again. Far off
a whip-poor-will plied his notes incessantly. It was that silent time
between 1 and 3.

FURTHERMORE

February 19, 1880.—Just before 10 P.M. cold and entirely clear
again, the show overhead, bearing southwest, of wonderful and
crowded magnificence. The moon in her third quarter—the
clusters of the Hyades and Pleiades, with the planet Mars
between—in full crossing sprawl in the sky the great Egyptian X,
(Sirius, Procyon, and the main stars in the constellations of the
Ship, the Dove, and of Orion;) just north of east Bootes, and in
his knee Arcturus, an hour high, mounting the heaven,
ambitiously large and sparkling, as if he meant to challenge with
Sirius the stellar supremacy.

With the sentiment of the stars and moon such nights I get
all the free margins and indefiniteness of music or poetry, fused
in geometry's utmost exactness.

FULL-STARR'D NIGHTS

May 21.—Back in Camden. Again commencing one of those unusually transparent, full-starr'd, blue-black nights, as if to show that however lush and pompous the day may be, there is something left in the not-day that can outvie it. The rarest, finest sample of long-drawn-out clear-obscure, from sundown to 9 o'clock. I went down to the Delaware, and cross'd and cross'd. Venus like blazing silver well up in the west. The large pale thin crescent of the new moon, half an hour high, sinking languidly under a bar-sinister of cloud, and then emerging. Arcturus right overhead. A faint fragrant sea-odor wafted up from the south. The gloaming, the temper'd coolness, with every feature of the scene, indescribably soothing and tonic—one of those hours that give hints to the soul, impossible to put in a statement. (Ah, where would be any food for spirituality without night and the stars?) The vacant spaciousness of the air, and the veil'd blue of the heavens, seem'd miracles enough.

As the night advanc'd it changed its spirit and garments to ampler stateliness. I was almost conscious of a definite presence, Nature silently near. The great constellation of the Water-Serpent stretch'd its coils over more than half the heavens. The Swan with outspread wings was flying down the Milky Way. The northern Crown, the Eagle, Lyra, all up there in their places. From the whole dome shot down points of light, rapport with me, through the clear blue-black. All the usual sense of motion, all animal life, seem'd discarded, seem'd a fiction; a curious power, like the placid rest of Egyptian gods, took possession, none the less potent for being impalpable. Earlier I had seen many bats, balancing in the luminous twilight, darting their black forms hither and yon over the river; but now they altogether disappear'd. The evening star and the moon had gone. Alertness and peace lay calmly couching together through the fluid universal shadows.

BIVOUAC ON A MOUNTAIN SIDE

I see before me now a traveling army halting,
Below a fertile valley spread, with barns and the orchards of
    summer,
Behind, the terraced sides of a mountain, abrupt, in places
    rising high,
Broken, with rocks, with clinging cedars, with tall shapes
    dingily seen,
The numerous camp-fires scatter'd near and far, some away up
    on the mountain,
The shadowy forms of men and horses, looming, large-sized,
    flickering,
And over all the sky—the sky! far, far out of reach, studded,
    breaking out, the eternal stars.

LOOK DOWN FAIR MOON

Look down fair moon and bathe this scene,
Pour softly down night's nimbus floods on faces
    ghastly, swollen, purple,
On the dead on their backs with arms toss'd wide,
Pour down your unstinted nimbus sacred moon.

A SILENT NIGHT RAMBLE

October 20th.—To-night, after leaving the hospital at 10 o'clock,
(I had been on self-imposed duty some five hours, pretty closely
confined,) I wander'd a long time around Washington. The night
was sweet, very clear, sufficiently cool, a voluptuous half-moon,
slightly golden, the space near it of a transparent blue-gray tinge.
I walk'd up Pennsylvania avenue, and then to Seventh street, and
a long while around the Patent-office. Some-how it look'd
rebukefully strong, majestic, there in the delicate moonlight. The
sky, the planets, the constellations all so bright, so calm, so
expressively silent, so soothing, after those hospital scenes. I
wander'd to and fro till the moist moon set, long after midnight.

A CLEAR MIDNIGHT

This is thy hour O Soul, thy free flight into the wordless,
Away from books, away from art, the day erased, the lesson done,
Thee fully forth emerging, silent, gazing, pondering the themes
      thou lovest best,
Night, sleep, death and the stars.

THINKING AND SINGING ABOUT THE EARTH

A THOUGHT OF THE CLEF OF ETERNITY

What can the future bring me more than I have?
Do you suppose I wish to enjoy life in other spheres?

I say distinctly I comprehend no better sphere than this earth,
I comprehend no better life than the life of my body.

I do not know what follows the death of my body,
But I know well that whatever it is, it is best for me,
And I know well that whatever is really Me shall live just as much
    as before.

I am not uneasy but I shall have good housing to myself,
But this is my first—how can I like the rest any better?
Here I grew up—the studs and rafters are grown parts of me.

I am not uneasy but I am to be beloved by young and old men,
    and to love them the same,
I suppose the pink nipples of the breasts of women with whom I
    shall sleep will touch the side of my face the same,
But this is the nipple of a breast of my mother, always near and
    always divine to me, her true child and son, whatever comes.

I suppose I am to be eligible to visit the stars, in my time,
I suppose I shall have myriads of new experiences—and that the
    experience of this earth will prove only one out of
    myriads;
But I believe my body and my Soul already indicate those
    experiences,
And I believe I shall find nothing in the stars more majestic and
    beautiful than I have already found on the earth,
And I believe I have this night a clew through the universes,
And I believe I have this night thought a thought of the clef of
    eternity.

From A SONG OF JOYS

O for the voices of animals—
    O for the swiftness and balance of fishes!
O for the dropping of raindrops in a song!
O for the sunshine and motion of waves in a song!

From A SONG OF THE ROLLING EARTH

The earth does not exhibit itself nor refuse to exhibit itself,
    possesses still underneath,
Underneath the ostensible sounds, the august chorus of heroes,
    the wail of slaves,
Persuasions of lovers, curses, gasps of the dying, laughter of
    young people, accents of bargainers,
Underneath these possessing words that never fail.

To her children the words of the eloquent dumb great mother
    never fail,
The true words do not fail, for motion does not fail and
    reflection does not fail,
Also the day and night do not fail, and the voyage we pursue
    does not fail.

THE COMMON EARTH, THE SOIL

The soil, too—let others pen-and-ink the sea, the air, (as I sometimes try)—but now I feel to choose the common soil for theme—naught else. The brown soil here, (just between winter-close and opening spring and vegetation)—the rain-shower at night, and the fresh smell next morning—the red worms wriggling out of the ground—the dead leaves, the incipient grass, and the latent life underneath—the effort to start something— already in shelter'd spots some little flowers—the distant emerald show of winter wheat and the rye-fields—the yet naked trees, with clear interstices, giving prospects hidden in summer—the tough fallow and the plow-team, and the stout boy whistling to his horses for encouragement—and there the dark fat earth in long slanting stripes upturn'd.

NOVEMBER 8, '76

The forenoon leaden and cloudy, not cold or wet, but indicating both. As I hobble down here and sit by the silent pond, how different from the excitement amid which, in the cities, millions of people are now waiting news of yesterday's Presidential election, or receiving and discussing the result—in this secluded place uncared-for, unknown.

THE CALMING THOUGHT OF ALL

That coursing on, whate'er men's speculations,
Amid the changing schools, theologies, philosophies,
Amid the bawling presentations new and old,
The round earth's silent vital laws, facts, modes continue.

From SONG AT SUNSET

Good in all,
In the satisfaction and aplomb of animals,
In the annual return of the seasons,
In the hilarity of youth,
In the strength and flush of manhood,
In the grandeur and exquisiteness of old age,
In the superb vistas of death.

Wonderful to depart!
Wonderful to be here!
The heart, to jet the all-alike and innocent blood!
To breathe the air, how delicious!
To speak—to walk—to seize something by the hand!
To prepare for sleep, for bed, to look on my rose-color'd flesh!
To be conscious of my body, so satisfied, so large!
To be this incredible God I am!
To have gone forth among other Gods, these men and women I love.

Wonderful how I celebrate you and myself!
How my thoughts play subtly at the spectacles around!
How the clouds pass silently overhead!
How the earth darts on and on! and how the sun, moon,
        stars, dart on and on!
How the water sports and sings! (surely it is alive!)
How the trees rise and stand up, with strong trunks, with
        branches and leaves!
(Surely there is something more in each of the trees,
        some living soul.)

A JULY AFTERNOON BY THE POND

The fervent heat, but so much more endurable in this pure air—
the white and pink pond-blossoms, with great heart-shaped
leaves; the glassy waters of the creek, the banks, with dense
bushery, and the picturesque beeches and shade and turf; the
tremulous, reedy call of some bird from recesses, breaking the
warm, indolent, half-voluptuous silence; an occasional wasp,
hornet, honey-bee or bumble (they hover near my hands or face,
yet annoy me not, nor I them, as they appear to examine, find
nothing, and away they go)—the vast space of the sky overhead
so clear, and the buzzard up there sailing his slow whirl in
majestic spirals and discs; just over the surface of the pond, two
large slate-color'd dragon-flies, with wings of lace, circling and
darting and occasionally balancing themselves quite still, their
wings quivering all the time, (are they not showing off for my
amusement?)—the pond itself, with the sword-shaped calamus;
the water snakes—occasionally a flitting blackbird, with red dabs
on his shoulders, as he darts slantingly by—the sounds that bring
out the solitude, warmth, light and shade—the quawk of some
pond duck—(the crickets and grasshoppers are mute in the noon
heat, but I hear the song of the first cicadas;)—then at some
distance the rattle and whirr of a reaping machine as the horses
draw it on a rapid walk through a rye field on the opposite side
of the creek—(what was the yellow or light-brown bird, large as a
young hen, with short neck and long-stretch'd legs I just saw, in
flapping and awkward flight over there through the trees?)—the
prevailing delicate, yet palpable, spicy, grassy, clovery perfume to
my nostrils; and over all, encircling all, to my sight and soul, the
free space of the sky, transparent and blue—and hovering there
in the west, a mass of white-gray fleecy clouds the sailors call
"shoals of mackerel"—the sky, with silver like locks of toss'd hair,
spreading, expanding—a vast voiceless, formless simulacrum—
yet may-be the most real reality and formulator of everything—
who knows?

From SONG OF MYSELF

The spotted hawk swoops by and accuses me, he complains of
    my gab and loitering.

I too am not a bit tamed, I too am untranslatable,
I sound my barbaric yawp over the roofs of the world.

The last scud of day holds back for me,
It flings my likeness after the rest and true as any on
    the shadow'd wilds,
It coaxes me to the vapor and the dusk.

I depart as air, I shake my white locks at the runaway sun,
I effuse my flesh in eddies, and drift it in lacy jags.

I bequeath myself to the dirt to grow from the grass I love,
If you want me again look for me under your boot-soles.

You will hardly know who I am or what I mean,
But I shall be good health to you nevertheless,
And filter and fibre your blood.

Failing to fetch me at first keep encouraged,
Missing me one place search another,
I stop somewhere waiting for you.

H≡RON DANC≡

Heron Dance is a nonprofit 501(c)3 organization founded in 1995 by artist Roderick MacIver and run today with his wife Ann O'Shaughnessy. It is a work of love, an effort to produce something that is thought-provoking and beautiful. Through our website, quarterly journal, workshops, free weekly e-newsletter and watercolors, *Heron Dance* celebrates the seeker's journey and the beauty and mystery of the natural world.

We invite you to visit us at www.herondance.org to view the many nature watercolors by Roderick MacIver and to browse the hundreds of pages of book excerpts, poetry, essays and interviews of authors and artists. In our gallery store, we offer *Heron Dance* notecards, Limited Edition prints, and originals as well as dozens of hard-to-find books, music and films.

To receive our free weekly e-newsletter—*A Pause for Beauty*—which features a new watercolor and a poem or excerpt, just click on the *Pause for Beauty* link found on our website or contact us at the number below.

www.herondance.org • 888-304-3766
heron@herondance.org

A Death on the Barrens by George Grinnell

Five young men canoe through Canada's arctic and must find their way home, after the death of their leader, Art Moffat, from hypothermia. Winter closes in, the group runs out of food. The book is both an account of a journey through then unmapped northern lakes and rivers, and a story of the spiritual awakening of the young men on the trip. A Death on the Barrens was first published in 1996, and quickly sold out. This second edition contains watercolors by Roderick MacIver. 192 pages.

#6075   A Death on the Barrens – $19.95

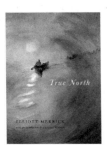

True North by Elliott Merrick
with an introduction by Lawrence Millman

In 1929, at the age of 24, Elliott Merrick left his position as an advertising executive in New Jersey and headed up to Labrador to work as an unpaid volunteer for the Grenfell Mission. In 1933 he wrote True North about his experiences in the northern wilderness, living and working with trappers, Indians and with the nurse he met and married in a remote community. The book describes the hard work and severe conditions, along with the joy and friendship he and his wife experienced. 320 pages

#6078   True North – $19.95

Sleeping Island:
A Journey to the Edge of the Barrens
by P.G. Downes

In Sleeping Island, Prentice G. Downes records a journey made in 1939 of a North that was soon to be no more, a landscape and a people barely touched by the white man. His respect for the Native Indians and the Inuit and their ways of life, and his love of their land, shine through this richly descriptive work. With the kind permission of the Downes family, Heron Dance has republished this book. 288 pages.

#6056   Sleeping Island – $19.95

Forest Under My Fingernails
Reflections and Encounters on the Long Trail

Years ago we excerpted this book about Walt McLaughlin's wilderness trek. The book sold out, but has recently been reprinted. His reflections and encounters are beautifully told. We highly recommend it. 192 pages.

#6013   Forest Under My Fingernails – $15.95

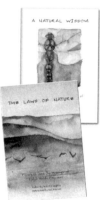

A Natural Wisdom—Gleanings from the Journals of Henry David Thoreau

Walt McLaughlin selects 80 thought-provoking and insightful entries from Thoreau's journals. 60 pages.

#6019   A Natural Wisdom – $10.00

The Laws of Nature—Excerpts from the Writings of Ralph Waldo Emerson

Another inspiring collection edited by Walt McLaughlin. 35 pages.

#6018   The Laws of Nature – $7.95

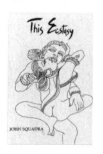

This Ecstasy by John Squadra

This courageous and beautiful book of poems explores, with simplicity, the truths of love and a spiritual life. Some poems are very erotic. Some poems expose the truths of life we all share.

#6043   This Ecstasy – $10.95

Heron Dance Book of Love and Gratitude

Heron Dance celebrates the open heart and the beauty and mystery that surround us with this book of poetry, book and interview excerpts. 48 watercolors by Rod MacIver and selections from the written works of Helen Keller, Dostoevsky, and Henry Miller, among many others. 80 pages.

#1602   Heron Dance Book of Love and Gratitude – $12.95

DATE DUE			